PROFESSIONAL STUDIO TECHNIQUES
IMAGING ESSENTIALS

Luanne Seymour Cohen ▪ Russell Brown ▪ Tanya Wendling

D0534130

Adobe Press
Mountain View, California

Copyright © 1993 Adobe Systems Incorporated. All rights reserved.

No part of this publication may be reproduced, stored in a retrieval system, or transmitted, in any form or by any means, electronic, mechanical, photocopying, recording, or otherwise, without the prior written permission of Adobe Systems Incorporated.

Patents Pending.

Library of Congress Catalog No.: 93-80007

ISBN: 1-56830-051-4

First Printing: September 1993   2 3 4 5 6 7 8 9 10

The information in this book is furnished for informational use only, is subject to change without notice, and should not be construed as a commitment by Adobe Systems Incorporated. Adobe Systems Incorporated assumes no responsibility for any errors or inaccuracies that may appear in this book. The software described in this book is furnished under license and may only be used or copied in accordance with the terms of such license.

PostScript™ is a trademark of Adobe Systems Incorporated ("Adobe"), registered in the United States and elsewhere. PostScript can refer both to the PostScript language as specified by Adobe and to Adobe's implementation of its PostScript language interpreter.

Any references to "PostScript printers," "PostScript files," or "PostScript drivers" refer, respectively, to printers, files and driver programs written in or supporting the PostScript language. References in this book to the "PostScript language" are intended to emphasize Adobe's standard definition of that language.

Adobe, the Adobe Press logo, Adobe Accurate Screens, Adobe Acrobat, Adobe Dimensions, Adobe Illustrator, Adobe Photoshop, Adobe Premiere, Adobe Separator, Adobe Type Manager, Classroom in a Book, Minion, Myriad, and PostScript are trademarks of Adobe Systems Incorporated, which may be registered in certain jurisdictions. Spectrum is a trademark and Cantoria is a registered trademark of The Monotype Corporation registered in the US Patent & Trademark Office and elsewhere. Cosmos is a trademark of H. Berthold AG. Helvetica is a trademark of Linotype-Hell AG and/or its subsidiaries. ITC American Typewriter, ITC Berkeley Oldstyle, and ITC Avant Garde are registered trademarks of International Typeface Corporation. Macintosh is a registered trademark of Apple Computer, Inc. Pagemaker and Freehand are registered trademarks of Aldus Corporation. Scitex is a registered trademark, and Dolev is a trademark of Scitex Corporation. Serpentine is a trademark of V.G.C. Revue is a trademark of Esselte Pendaflex Corporation in the U.S.A., of Letraset Canada Ltd. in Canada and of Esselte Letraset Ltd. elsewhere. Quark and Xpress are registered trademarks of Quark, Incorporated.

*Pantone, Inc.'s check-standard trademark for color reproduction and color reproduction materials.

Printed in the United States of America.

Published simultaneously in Canada.

Published and distributed to the trade by Hayden, a division of Prentice Hall Computer Publishing. For information, address Hayden, 11711 N. College Avenue, Carmel, IN 46032   1-800-428-5331.

Credits

Authors: Luanne Seymour Cohen, Russell Brown, Tanya Wendling

Editors: Tanya Wendling, Judy Walthers von Alten

Designer: Lisa Jeans

Illustration: Anita Jamshidi, Hung Yin-Yin

Cover Design: Eric Baker

Cover Illustration: Louis Fishauf

Color Correction Consultants: Jim Rich, Vince DiPaola

Other Contributors: Ellen Ablow, Patrick Ames, Rita Amladi, Fred Barling, Dean Bernheim, Lyn Bishop, Desirée Blackman, Matt Brown, Jonathan Caponi, Susan Clem, Jean Covington, Lynn Dalton, Andy D'Ambruoso, Don Day, Laura Dower, Terry Erb, Steffen Fanger, Erik-Paul Gibson, Ron Gross, Mark Hamburg, Joe Holt, Kim Isola, David Jacobs, John Knoll, Julieanne Kost, Peggy Larkin, Elizabeth McEnroe, Sean McKenna, Laurcna Katz Morton, Tim Myers, Mike Ouslander, David Rodenborn, Jim Ryan, Denise Salles, Mark Schumann, Scott Smith, Cindy Stief, Laurie Szujewska, Eric Thomas, John Warnock, Lisa Wheeler

Photography: Mark Boscacci (p. 82, 84); Michelle Clement (pp. 91, 95); Luanne Cohen (p. 26, 37, 42, 58, 59, 63, 84, 86); Jessica Cohen (p. 40); ColorBytes (p. 84); D'Pix Folio 1 (p. 70); Curtis Fukuda (pp. 68, 69, 70, 71, 80); Image Bank (p. 83); Lisa Jeans (pp. 23, 24, 59, 72, 107); NASA (p. 4); Rob Outwater (pp. 92, 94); PhotoDisc (pp. 8, 22, 24, 26, 30, 32, 42, 58, 62, 65, 89, 98, 101, 110); Dave Pratt (p. 110)

Contents

Introduction

Imaging Essentials is the second book in the Professional Studio Techniques series from Adobe Press, designed to help artists, illustrators, and designers achieve professional studio effects using a computer and Adobe software. Rather than describe how to use the software programs, these books are intended to serve as quick-reference "cookbooks" for artists familiar with the basic features of the programs. Each recipe consists of fully-illustrated, step-by-step instructions for creating a completed piece of artwork. In addition, the books include numerous tips on using the software efficiently, which are marked with the ∿ symbol throughout the book.

The first book in this series, *Design Essentials,* focused on two key Adobe software programs, Adobe Illustrator™ and Adobe Photoshop™. *Imaging Essentials* expands that scope by including two new programs from Adobe: a three-dimensional drawing program, Adobe Dimensions™, and a video-editing program, Adobe Premiere™. These two programs open worlds that were previously difficult, if not impossible, for artists and designers to enter.

If you own *Design Essentials*, you may wonder how the new software and new versions of the software affect the techniques in that book. In most cases, the effect is minimal. See the Appendix at the end of this book for complete update notes on *Design Essentials.*

Finally, although *Imaging Essentials* was created using Adobe software on the Macintosh® computer, the techniques in this book can be used with any computer that runs the required Adobe software or later versions of that software. The programs required for each technique are listed beneath the technique title. If you are using the software with a computer other than a Macintosh, see the Quick Reference Cards provided with your programs for the alternative keyboard shortcuts.

1 Three-Dimensional Artwork

Quick spheres with Adobe Illustrator

Software needed: Adobe Illustrator 5.0

You can make spheres using Adobe Dimensions or using the Adobe Photoshop technique described in Design Essentials. *If you don't have those programs, however, or if you just need a quick effect in Adobe Illustrator, you can use Adobe Illustrator's gradient fill tool to make spheres. The first method in this technique shows how to make a sphere using the oval tool and the gradient fill tool. The second method shows how to make a sphere with a colored background using just the gradient fill tool.*

Method 1

1. Select the oval tool, hold down the Shift key, and drag to draw a circle. If you know the diameter of the circle, click the mouse once (don't drag) to open the Oval dialog box. Enter the diameter in the Width and Height text boxes, and click OK.

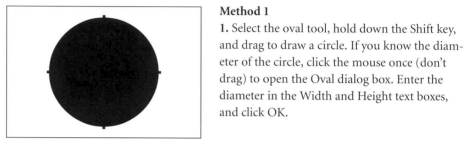

2. Next create a gradient fill for the sphere. Open the Gradient palette, click New, and name the gradient fill. Create a gradient fill with a highlight color on the left and a shadow color on the right. Click the Radial button.

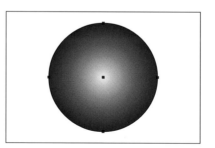

3. With the circle still selected, select the new gradient fill in the Paint Style palette. By default, the starting color, or highlight, is in the center of the selection.

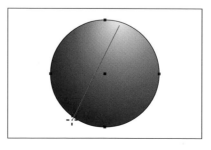

4. Select the gradient fill tool, and drag from the point where you want the highlight to the point where you want the shadow. Remember that these points can be outside the circle.

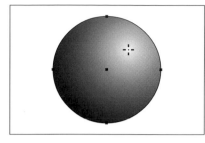

5. To experiment with other highlight positions, click with the gradient fill tool (don't drag) where you want the highlight to be. Illustrator will reposition the gradient fill automatically.

Method 2

1. Draw a rectangle or other shape as the background.

2. Create a gradient fill as described in step 2 of the previous method. (To use an existing gradient fill, select the fill name and click Duplicate.) Hold down the Option key and drag a copy of the rightmost triangle to the 95% point. (Note that this procedure does not work with 100% black.)

3. Now select the rightmost triangle. Adjust its color to a darker shade than that of the intermediate triangle. This will be the background color for the sphere.

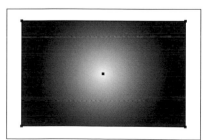

4. Select the rectangle or shape and use the Paint Style palette to paint the shape with the new gradient fill.

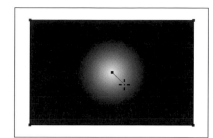

5. Click the gradient fill tool, and drag from the center of the highlight to where you want the outer edge of the sphere. Make sure that the line is well within the boundaries of the background shape so that the whole sphere is visible.

6. If you want to experiment with different colored backgrounds, open the Gradient palette again and select the name of gradient fill you just created. Click the Duplicate button. Select the rightmost triangle and change the color. Name the new gradient fill.

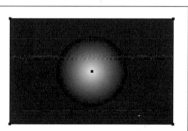

7. With the background shape still selected, select the new gradient fill in the Paint Style palette. Because the gradient fill tool determines how all new gradient fills are applied, the sphere remains the same size.

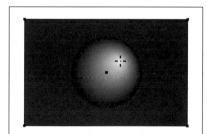

8. Click with the gradient fill tool to change the position of the highlight until the highlight is as you want it.

✦ *Adjusting the highlight*

To increase the amount of highlight color in a sphere created using the gradient fill tool, move the diamond above the gradient bar toward the right. To increase the shadow amount, move the diamond toward the left.

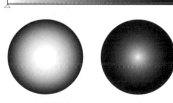

Highlight ◄········◇········► Shadow

More Highlight   More Shadow

Banners with type or graphics

Software needed: Adobe Illustrator 3.0, Adobe Dimensions 1.0

In this technique, you start with two pieces of artwork in Adobe Illustrator—the banner graphics and the banner line art. You then merge the artwork using the Artwork Mapping feature in Adobe Dimensions. The Artwork Mapping feature lets you easily add graphics to any three-dimensional object.

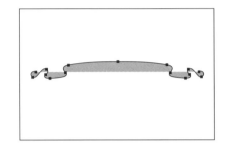

1. In Adobe Illustrator, use the pen tool to draw the curve that defines the bottom edge of the ribbon or banner. Make sure that the curve contains only smooth points; straight lines or corner points will cause segmenting of the ribbon. Paint the curve with a fill of a medium to light color and no stroke. Save the file with a suffix of *.ai*.

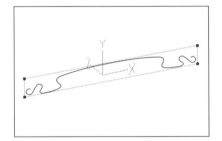

2. In a new Adobe Dimensions file, import (⌘-Shift-I) the ribbon artwork. (If you're using Adobe Illustrator 5.0, you can copy the Illustrator file to the Clipboard and paste it into Dimensions.) Make sure that the artwork is selected.

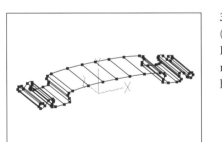

3. Choose Extrude from the Operations menu (⌘-Shift-E). Enter a value for the Absolute Depth of the extrusion. Because you will be rotating the banner, this value determines the height of the banner. Click OK.

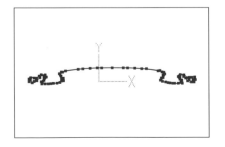

4. Change the view to Front (⌘1) and the perspective to Normal. You are now viewing the ribbon from below.

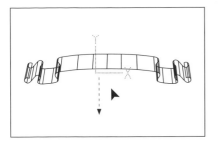

5. Using the rotate tool, hold down the Shift key and drag downward to rotate the ribbon on the *x* axis. When the ribbon face is positioned exactly as you want, release the mouse button and then the Shift key.

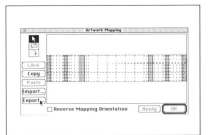

6. Create a Draft Render view (⌘Y) to preview the banner. Return to Artwork mode (⌘W) and adjust the rotation if desired.

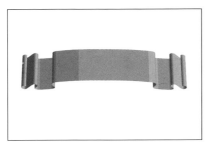

7. With the banner selected, choose Artwork Mapping from the Appearance menu (⌘F). A flat rendition of the banner with guidelines is displayed. The white areas represent the visible areas of the banner; the gray areas represent areas that are hidden by the banner folds. Click Export and save the guides as an Illustrator file as *banner.guides.ai*.

8. Open the *banner.guides.ai* file in Adobe Illustrator. Create the graphics or type for the banner and position it using the guides as reference.

9. Paint the type. Use light colors that won't disappear when black shading is added to them; the areas where the guides are close together will be shaded in the final artwork. With the type selected, choose Create Outlines from the Type menu. Save the file with the name *banner logo.ai*.

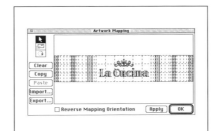

10. Return to the Adobe Dimensions file and make sure that the banner is selected. In the Artwork Mapping dialog box, click Import, and select the *banner logo.ai* file. Click Apply to preview the artwork. When you are satisfied with the position, click OK.

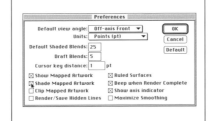

11. If you want the banner graphics to be shaded, select the Shade Mapped Artwork option in the Preferences dialog box (⌘K).

12. Preview your work by selecting Shaded Render (⌘-Shift-Y) using a low number of blend steps.

13. Now adjust the Lighting (⌘L) and Surface Properties (⌘I). Enter the correct number of blends for your artwork using the guidelines on pages 14–17. You may also want to change the perspective from Normal to Wide as shown in this example. Create a final shaded render, and export the file (⌘-Shift-S) as an Illustrator file.

Creating tubes, hoses, and wires

Software needed: Adobe Illustrator 3.0, Adobe Dimensions 1.0

ANS

RING

BUSY

since

Alexander Graham

ATND

BELL

HOLD

INNOVATIONS

2

4

TELECOMMUNICATIONS
CONFERENCE

Hartford Science Museum
Saturday, May 7, 1994
8:00 p.m.

A look into the past,
present, and future.

Usually when you extrude a form in Adobe Dimensions, you extrude a solid, closed shape. This technique shows how to extrude an open path to create open three-dimensional shapes. The key to getting good results with an open path is making sure that the path does not intersect itself. You begin this technique by creating a special bevel for the operation. Try other bevel shapes for some interesting results.

1. First you'll create a special bevel to use with the open path. You can create custom bevels in Adobe Illustrator. Open a new file in Illustrator. Select the oval tool, hold down the Option key, and click once. Enter the same value for the width and height of a small circle. In this example, we used 15 points.

2. Now you will cut the circle and add a segment to it so that Adobe Dimensions will recognize it as an open path bevel. Select the scissors tool, and click the bottom point of the circle.

3. Select the pen tool, and click the newly created point on the bottom of the circle. Move the pen tool just a few points above the point, hold down the Shift key, and click again to add a small segment to the circle. (Note that the example here has been enlarged by 200%.)

4. Name the bevel and save the file. If you want to use the bevel again for other objects, save the file in the Dimensions Bevel Library.

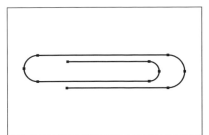

5. Open another new Illustrator file, and create an open path that doesn't intersect itself. (We drew this paper clip from the inside out.) If you're using Adobe Illustrator 5.0, copy the path to the Clipboard. If you're using an earlier version of Illustrator, save the file.

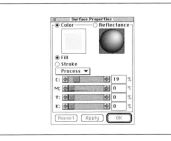

6. In Adobe Dimensions, open a new file. Paste or import (⌘-Shift-I) the path you created in step 5.

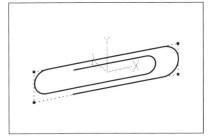

7. Choose Extrude from the Operations menu (⌘-Shift-E), click Relative Depth, and enter an extrusion amount based on the size of the bevel and path. (The Relative Depth value is a percentage of the object's widest dimension.) For our 15-point circle bevel, we used a value of 3%. Click the Bevel option, click Import, and select the bevel file you created in step 4. Click OK.

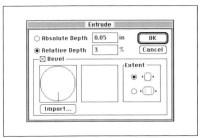

8. Before previewing the results, open the Surface Properties dialog box (⌘I), and make sure that the shape is painted with the color you want. If you change the fill color, don't forget to click Apply. In most cases, a stroke is not desirable on this type of artwork.

9. Choose Draft Render from the View menu (⌘Y) to preview the artwork.

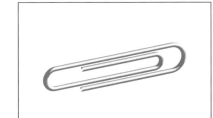

10. Adjust the Lighting (⌘L) and Surface Properties if desired. In this example, we selected a Plastic surface and changed the Ambient light to 16%, the Matte to 10%, and the Gloss to 12%.

11. See pages 14–17 for help determining how many blend steps to use in the shaded render. Enter the number of blends in the Surface Properties dialog box, and click Apply. Create a Shaded Render (⌘-Shift-Y).

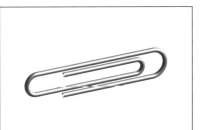

12. Save the file as an Adobe Dimensions file in case you need to rerender the object in the future. Then export the rendered file (⌘-Shift-S) as an Adobe Illustrator file.

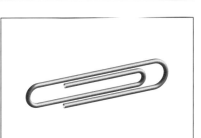

13. Return to Illustrator and open the file you exported from Dimensions. Preview the work.

14. If you're using Adobe Illustrator 5.0, you can use the Adjust Colors filter to make overall color changes. In this example, we decreased the cyan to 0% and slightly increased the magenta and yellow.

Creating a three-dimensional metal can

Software needed: Adobe Illustrator 5.0, Adobe Dimensions 1.0

In this technique, you create a metal can by creating and assembling three parts of the can. First, you create the metal lid. Then you create a cylinder for the body of the can and apply a label to it. Finally, you make the bottom of the can. Before you start, you should know the diameter and circumference of the can. This technique is an excellent way to make comps for package designs.

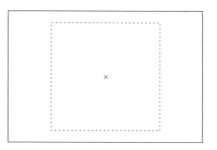

1. Before drawing the contour of the lid in Adobe Illustrator, you'll create guides to ensure that the lid will fit the cylinder. Select the rectangle tool, and click once to open the Rectangle dialog box. Enter the radius of the can as the height and width of the rectangle. Note the radius for later use; then click OK. Choose Guides/Make from the Object menu (⌘5).

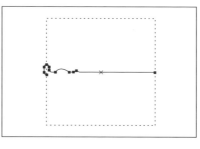

2. Use the pen tool to draw the contour of half the lid. Draw the lid as if you're holding it flat at eye level so that all you see is the contour of the top of the lid. Draw the contour of half of the lid from the left edge of the guide to the right edge. If your can lid has an overhanging lip, draw the lip so that it meets the can at the left guide.

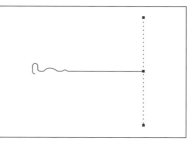

3. In Artwork view, paint the contour with a light blue or gray fill and no stroke. Unlock the guide (⌘7). Use the direct-selection tool to deselect the two right points of the rectangle, and then press Delete. The remaining line will serve as the axis of revolution in Dimensions. Save the file as *lidart.ai*.

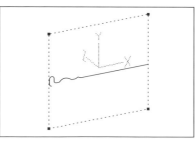

4. In Adobe Dimensions, open the *lidart.ai* file, and select the object.

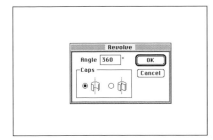

5. Choose Revolve from the Operations menu (⌘-Shift-R). Select the No Caps option and enter 360. Click OK.

6. Switch to Draft Render view (⌘Y). This step may take a while depending on the complexity of your artwork. The more curves and points in the contour, the more time required to render it. To render in the background so that you can work on other things simultaneously, hold down the Option key as you choose Draft Render.

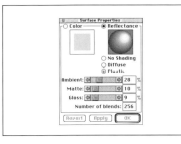

7. Now adjust the Surface Properties (⌘I). Click Reflectance, click Plastic, and adjust the highlight. The lower the Matte level, the whiter and shinier the object. The higher the Gloss value, the smaller the highlight. Use the Ambient slider to adjust the overall lightness. Record the values for use in step 15; then click OK.

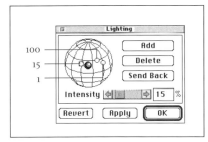

8. Use the Lighting dialog box (⌘L) to add one or two lights to the artwork. The intensity of the additional lights should be less than 100%. Record the lighting settings for use in step 15.

9. When you are satisfied with the lighting and reflectance, use the guidelines on pages 14–17 to determine the correct number of blends for the artwork. Then make the final shaded rendering (⌘-Shift-Y). Export the file (⌘-Shift-S) in Illustrator format with the name *lid.ai*. Save the file in Dimensions format with the name *lid.dim*.

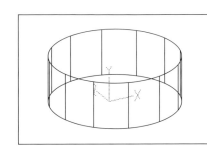

10. Now you will create the body of the can. Open a new Dimensions file. Select the cylinder drawing tool, and click once to open the dialog box. Enter the height of the cylinder and note the value for use in step 32. Enter the radius that you used to create the guide box in step 1. Click OK.

11. Choose Artwork Mapping from the Appearance menu (⌘F). Press the Tab key until the cylinder's side surface is selected and appears as a strip in the Artwork Mapping dialog box. Click Export, and save the file as *canguide.ai*. This file will serve as a guide for your can label.

12. Return to Illustrator, and open the *canguide.ai* file. Open the file you want to use for your label graphics. Select the label graphics, copy them, and paste them into the guide file. The label graphics should fit within the guides.

13. Before opening the label graphics in Dimensions, you must convert all type and stroked paths (such as rules) to outlines. Select any type, and choose Create Outlines from the Type menu. Select any rules, and choose Objects/Outline Stroked Path from the Filter menu. Save this new file in Adobe Illustrator 5.0 format as *label.ai*.

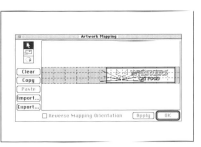

14. Return to the Dimensions file. With the cylinder selected, click Import in the Artwork Mapping dialog box, and import the *label.ai* file. Use the scale and selection tools in the Artwork Mapping dialog box to further adjust the size and position of the label graphics. Switch to Draft Render view, and click Apply to preview the results.

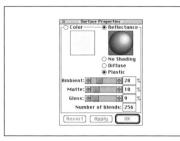

15. In the Surface Properties dialog box, enter the values you used for the lid in step 7. Using the guidelines on page 14–17, enter the correct number of blends for your final artwork. Click Apply. In the Lighting dialog box, add the lights and settings that you used in step 8.

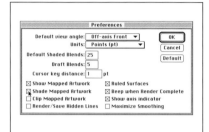

16. To ensure that shading is added to your label, choose Preferences from the Edit menu (⌘K), and select the Shade Mapped Artwork option.

17. Create a Shaded Render (⌘-Shift-Y). Export the file in Illustrator format as *body.ai*. Save the file as *body.dim*.

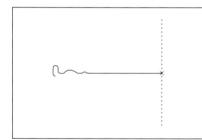
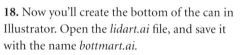

18. Now you'll create the bottom of the can in Illustrator. Open the *lidart.ai* file, and save it with the name *bottmart.ai*.

19. Select the contour, and click the reflect tool in the toolbox. Hold down the Option key, and click the point where the contour meets the guideline to open the Reflect dialog box. Make sure that the Horizontal Axis option is selected, and click OK.

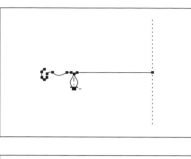

20. Most likely, the bottom of the can will be hidden in the final artwork, with the exception of the protruding lip around the edge. To save rendering and printing time, remove as many curves as possible from the contour. Use the delete-anchor-point tool to remove points; use the convert-direction-point tool to change curves to straight lines.

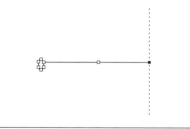

21. Save the file with the original axis of revolution guideline still in place.

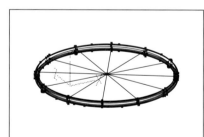

22. In Adobe Dimensions, open the *bottmart.ai* file. Select the contour.

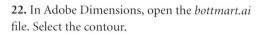

23. From the Operations menu, choose Revolve (⌘-Shift-R). Select the No Caps option and enter 360. Click OK.

24. Follow steps 6 through 9 to adjust the lighting and surface properties, and to render the final artwork. Save the file as *bottom.dim*, and export it in Illustrator format as *bottom.ai*.

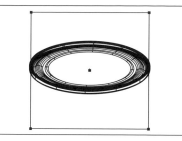

25. Now you will create a guide to assemble the parts in Adobe Illustrator. Open the *lid.ai* file in Illustrator, and resave it as *cancomp.ai*. In Artwork mode, select the lid. Then select the rectangle tool, hold down the Option key, and click the center point of the lid artwork. Create a box twice as wide as the radius of the can. Make the height of the rectangle taller than the can.

26. Choose Guides/Make from the Object menu (c5).

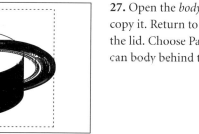

27. Open the *body.ai* file. Select the artwork and copy it. Return to the *cancomp.ai* file, and select the lid. Choose Paste In Back (cB) to place the can body behind the lid.

28. Drag the can body into position until it snaps to the guide. Then hold down the Shift key, and drag the can body by its bottom edge downward until the can body is just under the lip of the lid.

29. Preview to check that the can body is positioned correctly under the lid. If necessary, use the arrow keys on the keyboard to move the can body in small increments.

30. Return to Artwork mode, and open the *bottom.ai* file. Select the artwork and copy it. Return to the *cancomp.ai* file and select the lid and body. Choose Paste In Back from the Edit menu (cB) to place the can bottom behind the lid and can.

31. Drag the bottom of the can by its center point until it snaps to the center point of the lid. The lid and bottom should be perfectly aligned.

32. With the can bottom still selected, hold down the Option key, and click the selection tool in the toolbox to open the Move dialog box. In the Distance text box, enter the height that you noted in step 10. Enter –90 for the angle. Click OK.

33. Preview the results, and save the file.

᭡ *Centering objects in Adobe Dimensions*

A good way to align objects in Adobe Dimensions is to cut and paste them. For example, if you cut an object (cX), center the page (cH), and then paste the object (cV), the object is pasted at the 0,0,0 coordinates. Placing multiple objects at this location and then moving them enables you to align objects as precisely as possible.

Calculating blend steps in Adobe Dimensions

Software needed: Adobe Dimensions 1.0, Adobe Illustrator 3.0

Anyone who has created blends in a PostScript® language drawing program probably has had some problems with banding, or shade-stepping, in the final output. To some extent, the new gradient fill feature in Adobe Illustrator 5.0 has solved this problem. If you want to create blends using shapes, however, or if you are creating a shaded Adobe Dimensions file, you still need to specify the correct number of steps for your blend. If your blend contains too few steps or if the length of the blend is too long, banding will appear on the final print. If the blend contains too many steps, you may be wasting printing time and disk space. Use the charts or the formulas in this section to calculate precisely how many blend steps you need for your Dimensions object.

Decide on the output

To generate the smoothest blend possible in your Adobe Dimensions object, you first need to know how the object will be printed. For example, a 300-dots-per-inch (dpi) printer uses a line screen of 60 lines per inch (lpi) and prints up to 25 gray levels. This means that any more blend steps than 25 will be wasted. An imagesetter can print up to 256 gray levels—the exact number available depends on the resolution/line screen combination you use. To achieve the maximum number of gray levels with a line screen of 75, you must print at a resolution of 1200 dpi or higher. With a 150-lpi screen, you must print at a resolution of at least 2400 dpi.

Calculate the number of gray levels you can print

To determine the number of grays you can print, use the Grays Available column in the chart on page 17 or use the following formula:

$$\text{Number of grays} = \{\text{Resolution (dpi)} \div \text{line screen (lpi)}\}^2$$

If you've found that the resolution/line screen combination you are using to print your artwork does not produce 256 grays, you may be able to avoid banding by changing the number of steps in the Surface Properties dialog box.

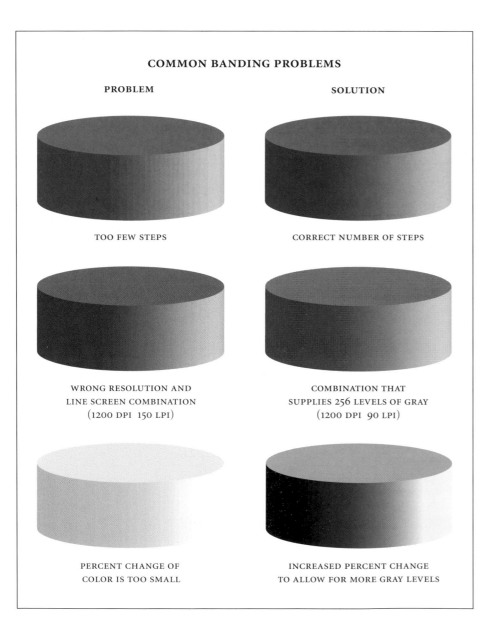

COMMON BANDING PROBLEMS

PROBLEM — SOLUTION

TOO FEW STEPS

CORRECT NUMBER OF STEPS

WRONG RESOLUTION AND LINE SCREEN COMBINATION (1200 DPI 150 LPI)

COMBINATION THAT SUPPLIES 256 LEVELS OF GRAY (1200 DPI 90 LPI)

PERCENT CHANGE OF COLOR IS TOO SMALL

INCREASED PERCENT CHANGE TO ALLOW FOR MORE GRAY LEVELS

STEPS TO A SMOOTHER BLEND

DIFFUSE

1. Determine the output resolution and line screen (page 14).
2. Figure out the number of gray levels available to your printer (page 14).
3. Determine the number of blend steps you need (page 15).
4. Make sure that the blend is not too long (page 17).

PLASTIC

1. Determine the output resolution and line screen (page 14).
2. Figure out the number of gray levels available to your printer (page 14).
3. Find the percent change in color in the shadow blend (page 16).
4. Find the percent change in color in the highlight blend (page 16).
5. Determine the number of blend steps you need (pages 16–17).
6. Make sure that the blend is not too long (page 17).

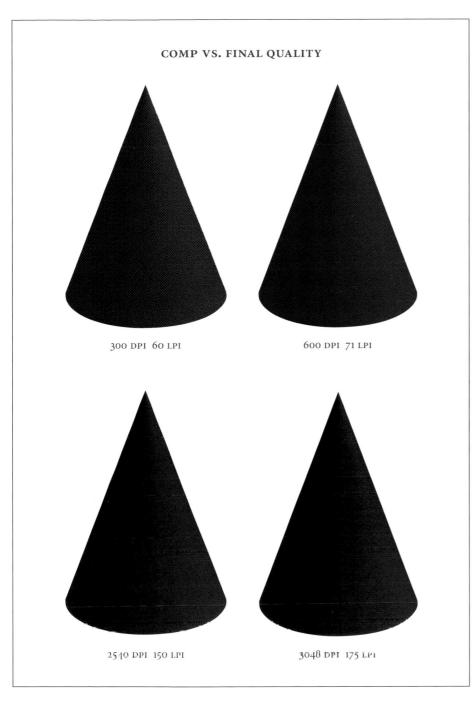

COMP VS. FINAL QUALITY

300 DPI 60 LPI

600 DPI 71 LPI

2540 DPI 150 LPI

3048 DPI 175 LPI

The number of grays you can print depends on your resolution and line screen. With most printers, increasing the line screen decreases the number of grays available. The examples shown here illustrate the maximum line screen that can be used at common resolutions to achieve 256 levels of gray. The two examples on the top illustrate comp-quality output; the two examples on the bottom illustrate high-quality output.

Calculating the number of blend steps for diffuse reflectance

With objects created in Adobe Dimensions, the color change in the blend depends on the lighting and reflectance properties of the object. For objects with diffuse lighting, Dimensions simply adds black to the original color of the object to shade the object and create the three-dimensional effect. Therefore for these objects, the change in color in the blend is determined by the change in black. With 0% ambient light, the black in the shadow will range from 0% to 100%. With 20% ambient light, the black will range from 0% to 80%. (The original color is not affected by ambient light.) Use the chart below to estimate the number of steps you need for a diffused object. For a more precise number, calculate the number of steps available for your diffuse blend using this formula:

Number of steps = Number of grays available × (100 − Ambient light %)

NUMBER OF BLEND STEPS FOR DIFFUSED OBJECTS		
AMBIENT LIGHT PERCENTAGE	COMP QUALITY	HIGH QUALITY
0	25	256
10	23	231
20	20	205
30	18	179
40	15	154
50	13	128
60	10	102
70	8	77
80	5	51
90	3	26
100	0	0

Find the percentage of ambient light you are using. For diffused objects, the number of steps you need in your blend depends on the ambient light and on your output quality. A resolution of 1200 dpi or higher is considered high quality; if you're printing at a lower resolution, use the Comp Quality column.

Calculating the number of blend steps for plastic reflectance

When an object is assigned a plastic reflectance, Adobe Dimensions does more than just add black to the original color. In this case, Dimensions creates two separate gradations: the shadow blend, which ranges from the original color to the original color plus black; and the highlight blend, which ranges from 100% to 0% of the original color. The number of blend steps you enter is split evenly between the two blends. This means that if the highlight blend goes from 0% to 100% cyan, for example, you might need 256 steps for that blend alone, but you will be able to produce only 128.

To determine the correct number of steps for the two blends, you must first figure out which blend contains the largest percent change in color. You can do this by referring to the two charts below. Use the chart on the left to find the percent change in the shadow blend, as determined by the Ambient Light percentage you've entered in the Surface Properties dialog box. Use the chart on the right to find the percent change in the highlight blend, as determined by the Matte percentage you're using and the highest percentage of C, M, Y, or K in the object's base color. Compare the percent change in the highlight with the percent change in the shadow and use the larger of the two numbers in the following formula:

Number of steps = Number of grays available × Percent change in color × 2

Another way to figure out the percent change in a blend color is to subtract the lower value from the higher value—for example, a blend between 50% black and 100% black indicates a 50% change in color. When blending process color combinations, identify the largest percent change in the four process colors. For example, a blend from 10% yellow and 50% magenta to 80% yellow and 70% magenta indicates a 70% change, dictated by the change in yellow.

When you have calculated the number of steps, enter the value in the Surface Properties dialog box. Entering fewer blends steps than this value will give you fewer gray levels than are available, and so may cause banding. Entering more blend steps than this value will increase the file size with no improvement in the printed output.

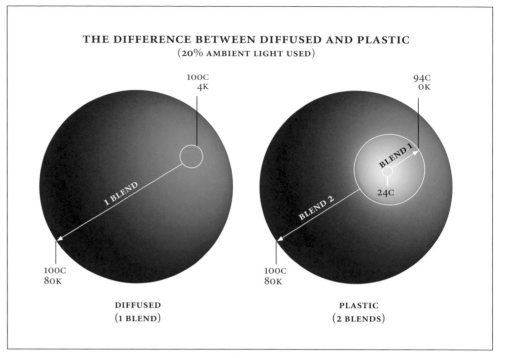

THE DIFFERENCE BETWEEN DIFFUSED AND PLASTIC
(20% AMBIENT LIGHT USED)

DIFFUSED
(1 BLEND)

PLASTIC
(2 BLENDS)

PERCENT CHANGE IN THE SHADOW	
AMBIENT LIGHT PERCENTAGE	BLACK PERCENTAGE CHANGE
0	97
10	87
20	77
30	67
40	57
50	47
60	37
70	27
80	17
90	7
100	0

The percent change in the shadow blend is determined by the ambient light percentage you're using. This value indicates how much black is added to create the shadow.

PERCENT CHANGE IN THE HIGHLIGHT											
MATTE PERCENTAGE	HIGHEST PERCENTAGE OF PROCESS COLOR										
	100	90	80	70	60	50	40	30	20	10	0
0	95	85	76	66	57	47	38	28	19	9	0
10	85	77	68	58	51	43	34	25	17	9	0
20	76	68	61	53	45	38	30	23	15	8	0
30	66	60	53	46	40	33	27	20	13	7	0
40	57	51	46	40	34	28	23	17	11	6	0
50	47	43	38	33	28	24	19	14	9	5	0
60	38	34	30	27	23	19	15	11	8	4	0
70	28	26	23	20	17	14	11	9	6	3	0
80	19	17	15	13	11	9	8	6	4	2	0
90	10	9	8	7	6	5	4	3	2	1	0
100	0	0	0	0	0	0	0	0	0	0	0

The percent change in the highlight blend is determined by the Matte percentage you're using and by the highest of the process color values in your base color. For example, if your Matte value is 40% and the base color of your object is 80% cyan, 50% magenta, and 20% yellow, you use the 40% row and the 80% column to find the percent change in the highlight, which is 46.

NUMBER OF BLEND STEPS FOR PLASTIC OBJECTS (NUMBER OF GRAYS × PERCENT CHANGE × 2)																								
RESOLUTION DPI	LINE SCREEN LPI	GRAYS AVAILABLE	LARGEST PERCENT CHANGE IN BLEND																				
			0	5	10	15	20	25	30	35	40	45	50	55	60	65	70	75	80	85	90	95	100
300	60	25	0	3	5	8	10	13	15	18	20	23	25	28	30	33	35	38	40	43	45	48	50
600	71	71	0	7	14	21	28	36	43	50	57	64	71	78	85	92	99	107	114	121	128	135	142
1200	75	256	0	26	51	77	102	128	154	179	205	231	256	256	256	256	256	256	256	256	256	256	256
1200	90	178	0	18	36	53	71	89	107	125	142	160	178	196	214	231	249	256	256	256	256	256	256
1270	79	256	0	26	51	77	102	128	154	179	205	231	256	256	256	256	256	256	256	256	256	256	256
2400	150	256	0	26	51	77	102	128	154	179	205	231	256	256	256	256	256	256	256	256	256	256	256
2400	175	188	0	19	38	56	75	94	113	132	150	169	188	207	226	244	256	256	256	256	256	256	256
2540	160	252	0	25	50	76	101	126	151	176	202	227	252	256	256	256	256	256	256	256	256	256	256
3000	188	256	0	26	51	77	102	128	154	179	205	231	256	256	256	256	256	256	256	256	256	256	256
3600	225	256	0	26	51	77	102	128	154	179	205	231	256	256	256	256	256	256	256	256	256	256	256

Find the resolution and line screen combination you will use to print. Then find the largest percent change in color in the highlight and shadow blends. The number at the intersection of these values is the number of steps required to ensure that banding will not occur in your blend.

Check the length of the longest blend in the object

The last step to rendering an object for final output is to make sure that the blend is not too long to print without banding. If the length of a blend extends over a distance that is too long in proportion to the number of steps in the blend, banding can occur. To find out if your steps are smaller than the maximum size for a smooth blend, first measure or estimate the distance between the highlight and the shadow of the longest part of the blend. (With intricate or very curved blends, you will have to estimate.) Then use this formula to calculate the length of each step:

Step length = Blend length ÷ Number of steps

If the step length is 2.16 points (.03 inches or .0762 cm) or less, you should not get banding in the final output. If the step length is greater than 2.16 points, you may get banding, depending on the colors used in the blend—dark colors tend to cause more banding than light colors. If you can't decrease the length of the blend or change the number of steps, you can use the Add Noise filter in Adobe Photoshop to smooth the blend. (This procedure is described on page 41 of *Design Essentials,* the first book in the Professional Studio Techniques series.)

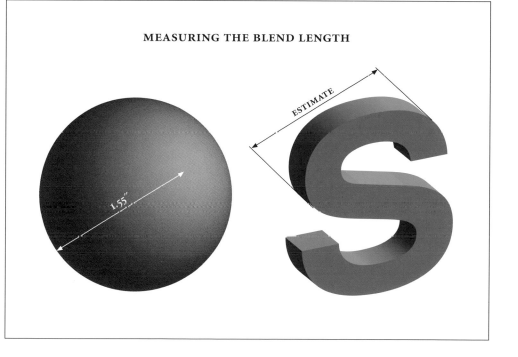

MEASURING THE BLEND LENGTH

Creating rounded three-dimensional containers

Software needed: Adobe Illustrator 3.0, Adobe Dimensions 1.0

This is a fairly simple technique to execute. The difficult part is getting just the right curve for the contour of the final object. Refer to the chart on pages 19–20 for curves that work for some commonly drawn containers. Remember that the shapes drawn here are symmetrical and circular. If you want to create an asymmetrical shape, such as a coffee mug with a handle, use this technique to create the coffee mug and then create the handle as a separate procedure.

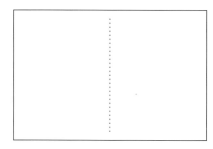

1. Before you draw the contour in Adobe Illustrator, make a guide for the center axis. Select the pen tool, and click to define the top of the axis; then hold down the Shift key, and click to define the bottom of the axis. With the line selected, choose Guides/Make from the Object menu (⌘5). (With Illustrator 3.0 or 4.0, choose Make Guides from the Arrange menu.)

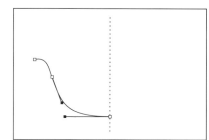

2. Draw half of the object's contour on one side of the guide, making sure that the line touches the guide and doesn't intersect itself. To save time and memory at the rendering stage, use the fewest number of points and curves possible to create the shape you want.

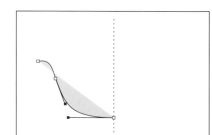

3. Select a fill color, keeping in mind that Adobe Dimensions will add black to shade the object. Paint the contour with the fill. For the best results, use a stroke of None. Strokes can't be shaded and may make the artwork less realistic. Save this file as *contour.ai.*

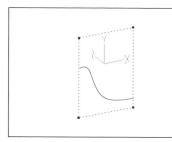

4. Now switch to Adobe Dimensions and import *contour.ai* (⌘-Shift-I). (If you're using Adobe Illustrator 5.0, you can copy the object to the Clipboard and paste it into the Dimensions file. Be sure to copy the guide along with the object.)

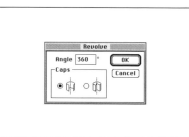

5. From the Operations menu, choose Revolve (⌘-Shift-R). Select the No Caps option, and enter 360. Click OK.

6. Make a Draft Render of the artwork (⌘Y). This step may take a while, depending on the complexity of the contour. To render the artwork in the background so that you can work on other things simultaneously, hold down the Option key as you select Draft Render.

7. Adjust the lighting (⌘L) and reflectance (⌘I). Refer to the examples at the end of this technique for help determining the settings to use. Enter the correct number of blends for your artwork using the guidelines on pages 14–17, and create the final Shaded Render (⌘-Shift-Y). Export the artwork as an Adobe Illustrator file for printing.

➷ Creating guides in Adobe Illustrator for importing into Adobe Dimensions

To create a guide, first draw a straight line with the pen tool; for the best results, draw the guide by clicking the pen tool rather than dragging. Then select the line, and choose Make Guides (⌘5). If you are using the guide as an axis of revolution in Dimensions, make sure that the end points of the path to be revolved are equidistant from the guide. If you are importing multiple objects with multiple guides, group each guide with its corresponding path.

CONTOUR	RENDER	APPEARANCE	CONTOUR	RENDER	APPEARANCE

Top-left (wine glass)

15 C
5 M
5 Y
0 K

Lighting
60
40
15
30
100
Add
Delete
Send Back
Intensity 100 %
Revert Apply OK

Surface Properties
Color Reflectance
No Shading
Diffuse
Plastic
Ambient: 20 %
Matte: 40 %
Gloss: 10 %
Number of blends: 256
Revert Apply OK

Top-right (cup)

WHITE

Lighting
100
31
Add
Delete
Send Back
Intensity 100 %
Revert Apply OK

Surface Properties
Color Reflectance
No Shading
Diffuse
Plastic
Ambient: 28 %
Matte:
Gloss:
Number of blends: 256
Revert Apply OK

Bottom-left (jar)

WHITE

50 C
100 M
10 Y
0 K

Lighting
100
60
50
60
Add
Delete
Bring Front
Intensity 60 %
Revert Apply OK

Surface Properties
Color Reflectance
No Shading
Diffuse
Plastic
Ambient: 20 %
Matte: 40 %
Gloss: 10 %
Number of blends: 256
Revert Apply OK

Bottom-right (pot)

30 C
100 M
90 Y
0 K

Lighting
100
50
40
30
Add
Delete
Send Back
Intensity 50 %
Revert Apply OK

Surface Properties
Color Reflectance
No Shading
Diffuse
Plastic
Ambient: 17 %
Matte:
Gloss:
Number of blends: 256
Revert Apply OK

2 Painting and Blending

Simulating graininess in a photograph

Software needed: Adobe Photoshop 2.5

Graininess is a mottled texture created by clumps of silver on negative film. This quality is usually seen in greatly enlarged photographs or in photographs shot at a fast film speed. The two techniques in this section describe how to simulate graininess using the Add Noise filter. With the first method, you add noise to only the Lightness channel of the image using Lab color mode. The second method produces a finer graininess: with this method, you add an equal amount of noise to the red and green components of an RGB image and then a lesser amount to the blue component.

METHOD 1

ORIGINAL	10 NOISE	25 NOISE	50 NOISE	75 NOISE

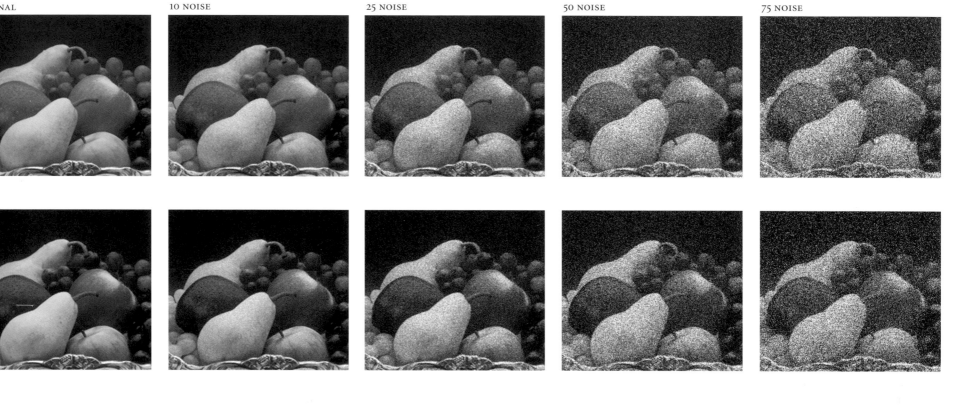

METHOD 2

R: 8 NOISE **G:** 8 NOISE **B:** 5 NOISE	**R:** 16 NOISE **G:** 16 NOISE **B:** 10 NOISE	**R:** 25 NOISE **G:** 25 NOISE **B:** 16 NOISE	**R:** 50 NOISE **G:** 50 NOISE **B:** 31 NOISE	**R:** 75 NOISE **G:** 75 NOISE **B:** 46 NOISE

Method 1

1. Open any color or black-and-white Adobe Photoshop file, and convert it to Lab color mode. Keep in mind that any large areas of white will be darkened with the "grain" that you add.

2. Choose Show Channels from the Window menu, and deselect the pencil icon next to the *a* and *b* channels. (The eye icon should be visible next to all four channels.) Setting up the Channels palette this way enables you to make changes to only the Lightness channel while viewing the effect on the composite image.

3. From the Filter menu, choose Noise/Add Noise. Refer to the examples on the facing page to determine the amount of grain you want in your image; then enter the amount, and select the Gaussian option. Click OK. To adjust the amount of noise, undo the filter effect (⌘Z) and try a different amount.

Method 2

1. Open an RGB file in Adobe Photoshop. (This method works only with RGB images.)

2. Select the red channel in the Channels palette (⌘1); then choose Noise/Add Noise from the Filter menu. Refer to the examples on the facing page to determine a noise amount (we used 8). Select the Gaussian option, and click OK.

3. Select the green channel (⌘2). Press ⌘F to reapply the filter using the same settings.

4. Select the blue channel (⌘3). Press ⌘-Option-F to open the dialog box for the last applied filter. Leave Gaussian selected, and change the Amount to 5. Click OK.

5. Return to the RGB channel (⌘0) to view the results.

✎ *Precise rotation in Adobe Photoshop*

When you need to know an exact rotation angle or to make a measurement, use the Info palette. To display the palette, choose Show Info from the Window menu.

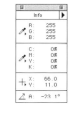

Select the object that you want to rotate and choose Rotate/Free from the Image menu. When the *A* value in the bottom of the Info palette displays the angle you want, release the mouse button, and click inside the selection to rotate the object.

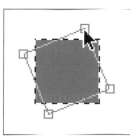

Creating black-and-white mezzotints

Software needed: Adobe Photoshop 2.5

A mezzotint is a random, nondirectional pattern produced in traditional printing by exposing an image to a specially designed halftone screen. This technique describes how to create a mezzotint pattern in Adobe Photoshop and then apply the pattern to your image as a halftone screen. You can print the final image in Bitmap mode for greater contrast and texture or in Grayscale mode for a softer, more detailed effect. Remember that bitmap images contain only two colors—black and white—and so are much smaller than grayscale images. For this reason, it's a good idea to print a proof while the image is still in Bitmap mode.

ORIGINAL GRAYSCALE IMAGE

RESOLUTION: 200 PPI   FILE SIZE: 99K

BITMAP MEZZOTINT

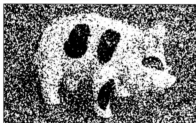

OUTPUT: 600 PPI   FILE SIZE: 112K

GRAYSCALE MEZZOTINT

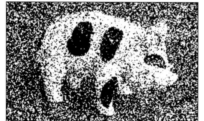

RESAMPLED FROM 600 PPI TO 200 PPI

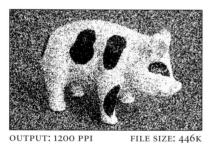

OUTPUT: 1200 PPI   FILE SIZE: 446K

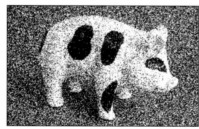

RESAMPLED FROM 1200 PPI TO 200 PPI

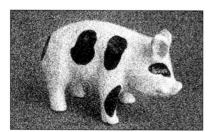

OUTPUT: 2400 PPI   FILE SIZE: 1.73MB

RESAMPLED FROM 2400 PPI TO 200 PPI

1. Open a grayscale file in Adobe Photoshop. For the best results, choose a file with a wide range of tones.

2. Look at the examples at the left, and determine which mezzotint texture you want. Choose Image Size from the Image menu, and adjust the resolution of the file to match the sample you chose.

3. Select everything in the file (⌘A) and copy it to the Clipboard (⌘C). (If your computer's memory is running low, skip this step and write down the size and resolution of the file for use in step 4.)

4. Select New from the File menu (⌘N). If you've copied the file to the Clipboard, the dialog box opens with the measurements of the document that you copied; otherwise, enter the measurements that you recorded in step 3. Select Grayscale mode, and click OK. From the Filter menu, choose Noise/Add Noise. Enter an amount of 100, select the Gaussian option, and click OK.

5. To increase the contrast and balance in the texture, select Map/Equalize from the Image menu (⌘E).

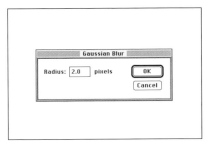

6. To soften the noise, choose Blur/Gaussian Blur from the Filter menu. Enter 2.0 in the Radius box, and click OK.

7. From the Edit menu, choose Select All (⌘A) and then Define Pattern. The mezzotint is now stored in memory as a custom pattern until you define another pattern or quit the program.

8. Next you'll increase the contrast in the original grayscale image. Select the original file from the Window menu, and deselect everything (⌘D). Choose Map/Equalize from the Image menu (⌘E). The image may look a little light; however, the mezzotint will darken it.

9. Choose Bitmap from the Mode menu. Make sure that the Output resolution matches the Input resolution. Select the Custom Pattern option, and click OK. Because you're holding the resolution constant while reducing the overall file size, the bitmap image will appear larger on your screen.

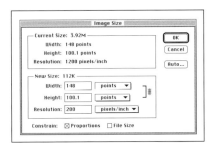

10. Double-click the hand tool to adjust the magnification to fit the window. Because of screen resolution limitations, it's a good idea to create a test print at this point. If the image resolution is higher than you need, use the Image Size dialog box to downsample the image. Make sure that the Constrain File Size check box is not selected in the Image Size dialog box.

Variation: Refer to the examples on the facing page to determine whether you want to convert the image to grayscale and then resample the image. Resampling in Grayscale mode converts the pixels to gray values and softens the overall effect. To convert the image to Grayscale, select Grayscale from the Mode menu. Leave the Size Ratio at 1, and click OK.

The file size of the image will now be what it was before you converted it to Bitmap mode. Choose Preferences/General from the File menu and make sure that the Interpolation option is Bicubic. If the Nearest Neighbor option is selected, the bitmap texture will remain the same and the soft gray values will not be introduced.

Choose Image/Image Size to reduce the resolution of the image. Make sure that the Constrain File Size option is deselected. Enter the new resolution, and click OK.

Resampling using Bicubic interpolation introduces gray pixels into the image, creating a softer and more varied texture. If you are satisfied with the effect and the new file size, save the image.

Creating an impressionist effect

Software needed: Adobe Photoshop 2.5

SANTA CRUZE SURFING CO.

CLASSES OFFERED FROM MAY TO SEPTEMBER

You can use the Lab Color mode in Adobe Photoshop to alter the lightness component of an image without affecting the color. This technique describes how to create an impressionist effect by adding noise to the Lightness channel of an image. To maintain image quality through the noise, the high-contrast areas in the image are outlined using the Find Edges filter; after adding noise to the image, the original image is partially restored by pasting it through a semitransparent mask. As you can see in this example, you can add a fair amount of noise to an image using this technique. Experiment with different noise amounts—with less noise, the technique produces a softer, watercolor-like effect.

1. Open an RGB image, and choose Lab Color from the Mode menu. Lab Color breaks the image into color channels *a* and *b* and Lightness channel *L*. Select the entire image (⌘A), and copy it to the Clipboard for later use. Deselect everything (⌘D).

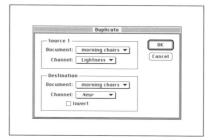

2. Before adding noise to the Lightness channel, you'll create the semitransparent mask to use at the end of the procedure. From the Image menu, choose Calculate/Duplicate. Duplicate the Lightness channel of the image file into a new channel of the same file (channel #4).

3. With channel #4 now the active window, choose Adjust and then Brightness/Contrast from the Image menu (⌘B). Decrease the contrast by dragging the white Contrast triangle to the left. (We used a value of –60.) The lower the contrast, the more even the transparency of the mask. Click OK.

4. Select the Lightness channel in the Channels palette (⌘1). From the Filter menu, choose Stylize/Find Edges. The Find Edges filter outlines all distinct edges in the Lightness channel.

5. Choose Noise/Add Noise from the Filter menu. Enter an Amount (we used 100 in this example), and click the Uniform option. The amount of noise you add depends on the resolution of the image and on the effect that you want. The higher the resolution of the image, the larger the amount of Noise you will need to notice a change.

6. Invert the image by selecting Map/Invert from the Image menu (⌘I).

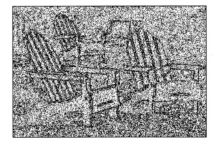

7. Apply the Add Noise filter again. (To repeat the last filter with the same values, press ⌘F.)

8. Reinvert the image by selecting Map/Invert from the Image menu (⌘I).

9. Select the composite Lab channel in the Channels palette (⌘0). Choose Load Selection from the Select menu to load the selection mask from channel #4.

10. Choose Paste Into from the Edit Menu. This pastes the original image that you copied to the Clipboard in step 1 into the selection mask.

Variation: To add more texture to the image, choose Load Selection from the Select menu to load channel #4 again.

Choose Inverse from the Select menu to invert the selection.

Now you will alter the Lightness channel only while viewing the effect in the Lab channel. Deselect the pencil icon next to the *a* and *b* channels in the Channels palette. A pencil icon should appear only next to the Lightness channel.

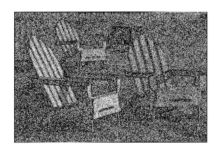

Apply the Add Noise filter again (⌘F); then deselect everything.

Creating a neon effect

Software needed: Adobe Photoshop 2.5

1. Design the neon type or graphics in Adobe Photoshop or Adobe Illustrator. Use only black and white paint because you will place this artwork into a channel in Adobe Photoshop.

2. In Adobe Photoshop, open or create a background for your neon graphics.

3. Choose New Channel from the Channels palette menu. Name the new channel *neon base art*.

4. Choose Place from the File menu, and select the artwork file you created in step 1. To scale the file, drag any of the four corner points. When the artwork is the size you want, click to place the graphic. Deselect the placed artwork (⌘D), and choose Map/Invert from the Image menu (⌘I) to create a negative of the image.

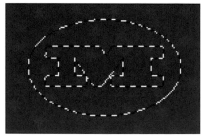

5. Return to the RGB channel (⌘0), and choose Load Selection from the Select menu. The graphic you placed in the channel is now the active selection.

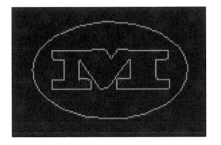

6. Choose Make Path from the Paths palette menu, and enter a Tolerance value in the Make Path dialog box. The higher the number, the less detailed the path will be. You may need to experiment with a few values to get the results you want.

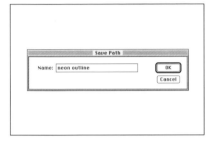

7. Choose Save Path from the Paths palette menu, name the path, and click OK. Think of this saved path as a sheet of tracing paper that you can reuse anytime.

8. The first stroke you add will create the "glow" from the neon light. Select a light color from the Colors palette. (We used white in this example.) Select the airbrush tool, open the Brushes palette, and choose a soft brush; set the mode to Normal and the Pressure to 50%. The size of the brush you choose depends on your image size and resolution.

9. With the airbrush tool still selected, choose Stroke Path from the Paths palette menu or press the Enter key. Because a painting tool is selected, the path is automatically stroked with the selected color and brush weight. (If the path is not stroked completely after choosing Stroke Path, double-click the airbrush tool and make sure that the fade-out value is 0.)

10. The next stroke will define the "edge" of the neon tube and should be a strong, bright color. Choose a color from the Colors palette, and select a brush from the Brushes palette. (If you want a wider glow around the neon, select an even smaller brush.) Press the Enter key to stroke the path.

11. The third stroke will create a rounded look by defining a brighter surface. Select a lighter tint of the color you chose for the neon tube, and a brush two sizes smaller than the one you chose in step 10. Press the Enter key to stroke the path. To view the results without the path selection showing, click the checkmark next to the path name in the Paths palette.

12. To add a very subtle highlight, choose a very small brush from the top row in the Brushes palette, reselect the path in the Paths palette, and stroke the path again with an even lighter tint of the color. This creates the effect of a very bright neon light.

Variation 1: To get a very different neon effect, choose Fill Path from the Paths palette menu before choosing Stroke Path in step 9. This example was created using Fill Path with a mode of Normal and an opacity of 100%.

Variation 2: Choose Fill Path as described in Variation 1, and fill the path using Screen mode. This example was created using Screen mode and an opacity of 100%.

∽ *Creating tints*

To easily select a tint of a color in RGB or CMYK mode, change the Colors palette to Lab or HSB mode. Select the color and adjust the L value slightly (or the S and B values slightly) to create a tint of the color.

Casting a transparent shadow

Software needed: Adobe Illustrator 5.0

Designers and illustrators commonly need semitransparent shapes for shadows that overlap other objects in their drawings. Although most drawing programs can't create true transparent objects, you can use Adobe Illustrator 5.0 to easily simulate transparency. Method 1 of this technique shows how to create a semitransparent shadow using solid colors and the Mix Hard filter. Method 2 shows how to create a more subtle effect using gradient fills and the gradient fill tool.

Method 1

1. Make sure that the artwork is sized, colored, and positioned as you want it. If any type falls within the shadow area, select the type and choose Create Outlines from the Type menu. If a stroked object falls in the shadow area, select the object and choose Objects/Outline Stroked Path from the Filter menu.

2. Create the shadow shape, and fill it with a tint of black. (We used 50% in this example.) Make sure that the shadow is in front of the objects it will shade and behind the object casting the shadow.

3. Select the shadow shape and lock it (⌘1). Locking the shape protects it while you edit the surrounding shapes.

4. Select the shape or shapes that fall within the shadow. If any two colors overlap beneath the shadow, choose Pathfinder/Divide Fill from the Filter menu to separate the overlapping colors. In this example, we applied Divide Fill to separate the dark brown fill drawn on top of the sand.

5. Unlock the shadow shape (⌘2). Hold down the Shift key and select the objects behind the shadow along with the shadow.

6. Choose Pathfinder/Mix Hard from the Filter menu to mix the overlapping colors.

Method 2
1. Follow steps 1 and 2 of the previous method. (It's not necessary to fill the shadow since you'll be filling it with a blend.) Select the shadow and all shapes behind it; from the Filter menu, choose Pathfinder/Divide Fill.

2. Open the Gradient palette, and click New. Select the leftmost triangle beneath the gradient bar. Select the eyedropper tool, hold down the Control key, and click a shape within the shadow area of the image to make that color the first color in your blend. Select the rightmost triangle, and define it as 100% black. Name the gradient fill after the leftmost color.

3. Repeat step 2 until you have created a gradient fill created for each color that falls within the shadow area. When you have finished, choose the direct-selection tool, hold down the Shift key, and select all shapes of one color. In this example, we selected the shapes in the sand area.

4. Use the Paint Style palette to fill the shapes with the corresponding gradient fill. It's not necessary to adjust the direction of the gradient fill yet.

5. Continue selecting all shapes of one color within the shadow area and filling them with the corresponding gradient fill.

6. Now select all shapes within the shadow. Choose the gradient fill tool, and drag to define the angle and length of the fills. In this example, we dragged from the top of the shadow shape to the bottom to create a blend from 100% color at the top of the shadow to 100% black at the bottom.

7. Experiment with the gradient fill tool to vary the heaviness of the shadow, using Hide Edges (⌘-Shift-H) to help preview the results. In this example, we started the gradient fill line outside the shadow and ended it well inside.

8. Deselect everything (⌘-Shift-A) when you are satisfied with the effect.

Making curved or circular gradations

Software needed: Adobe Illustrator 3.0

1. Create the shape that you will fill with a circular blend. For this shape, we drew a circle with a very thick stroke, deleted half the circle, and then chose Objects/Outline Stroked Path from the Filter menu. (If you're using Adobe Illustrator 3.0 or 4.0, create two concentric circles, delete their lower halves, and then join the end points. Leave the center point visible.)

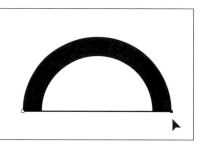

2. Use the pen tool to click an outside point on the circular shape. Then hold down the Shift key to constrain the angle of the line, and click the opposite point on the circle. The line should extend the diameter of the shape as if the shape were a complete circle.

3. If you're using Adobe Illustrator 5.0 and you deleted the center point in step 1, select the line and choose Attributes from the Object menu (⌘-Control-A). Select the Show Center Point option, and click OK. If you're using an earlier version of Illustrator, go on to the next step.

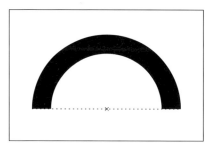

4. Define the line and center point as a guide (⌘5) for use when you rotate the blend. You are ready to construct the blend.

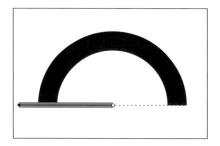

5. Use the pen tool to draw a straight line along the guide from the center point past the outside edge of the shape. Make sure that the line extends well outside of the shape. Stroke the line with the first color of your blend. The stroke weight you need depends on the size of the curved shape and the number of blends you create. (We used a stroke weight of 4 points.)

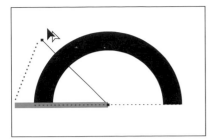

6. With the line selected, select the rotate tool and click the center point of the circle. Position the pointer on the end point of the line outside the curved shape. Hold down the Option key to copy the line, and drag along the curved shape to where you want the next color in the blend. Release the mouse button and then the Option key.

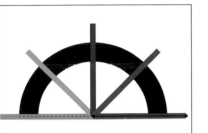

7. Paint the new line a different color.

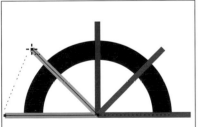

8. Repeat steps 6 and 7 until you have positioned the colors that you want in the blend around the circular shape.

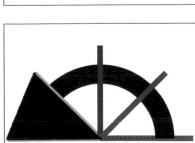

9. Select the first two lines you created. Select the blend tool (not the gradient fill tool), and click the outside point of the first line you created. Then click the outside point of the second line you created.

10. Illustrator calculates the numbers of steps needed for the blend and displays it in the Blend dialog box. Click OK. Because the lines are selected, the blend is obscured behind the lines. If the lines don't overlap, use the direct-selection tool to select the lines, increase the stroke weight in the Paint Style palette, and then repeat steps 9 and 10.

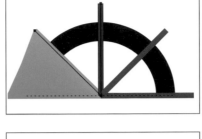

11. Choose Lock from the Arrange menu (⌘1) to lock the blend so that you can easily select the next blend elements. Select the second and third lines.

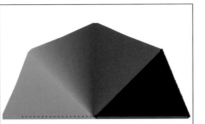

12. Repeat steps 9 through 11 for each pair of colored lines until you have covered the entire circular shape with blended lines.

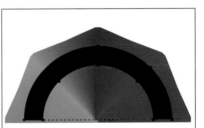

13. With the blends still locked, select the circular shape that will be filled with the blends, and choose Bring to Front (⌘=). If you're using Adobe Illustrator 3.0 or 4.0, select the shape, and choose Send to Back (⌘–).

14. Choose Hide from the Arrange menu (⌘3) to hide the circular shape. Then choose Unlock All from the Arrange menu (⌘2). Use the selection tool to select all blend lines, and choose Group from the Arrange menu (⌘G).

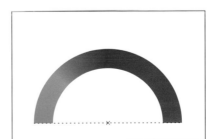

15. Choose Show All (⌘4). Select the blend group and the circular shape, and choose Masks/Make from the Object menu. If you're using Adobe Illustrator 3.0 or 4.0, select just the circular shape, and click the Mask option in the Paint Style dialog box. Group the mask, and then deselect (⌘-Shift-A) to view the result.

Painting and calculating

Software needed: Adobe Photoshop 2.5

Adobe Photoshop's calculate commands let you combine the pixel values of one file with the corresponding pixel values of another file. This technique shows how to copy a sketch into a new file, paint the sketch, and then merge it with the original file using different Calculate commands. Remember that any two files you combine must have exactly the same resolution and dimensions. Experiment with the Calculate commands until you find the effect you want. For more information on using the Calculate commands, see pages 72–77.

1. Open a grayscale image of a sketch you have created. The sketch can be made with traditional materials and then scanned as a grayscale file, or it can be created in Adobe Photoshop using the painting and drawing tools. Because you will create a color version of the same image, save this file with the suffix *.gray*.

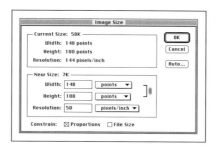

2. Choose Calculate/Duplicate from the Image menu. Duplicate the grayscale image into a new file. This gives you an unsaved copy of the file to experiment with, and leaves the original file intact.

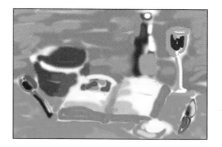

3. With the duplicated image active, choose Image Size from the Image menu. Write down the file's width, height, and resolution for use in step 6. Make sure that the Constrain File Size option is deselected, and reduce the resolution to between 30 pixels per inch (ppi) and 50 ppi. The low resolution will enable you to paint large areas of the image very quickly.

4. Convert the image to RGB mode, and select a color from the Colors palette. Select the paint brush or airbrush tool, and choose a large brush from the Brushes palette. Paint the areas that you want to appear in the final image. This file will define the colors and color areas of the final image.

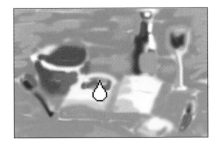

5. When you've finished painting, use the blur tool to soften any hard edges. Select the blur tool and set the pressure to 50% in the Brushes palette. Drag to blur the edges between colors.

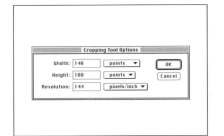

6. Because resampling in step 3 may have changed the dimensions of the file by 1 pixel, you must now use the cropping tool to ensure that the color and grayscale files are exactly the same size and resolution. Double-click the cropping tool, and enter the values that you recorded in step 3. Click OK.

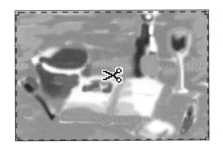

7. Select the entire image and crop it. Save the file with the suffix *.color*.

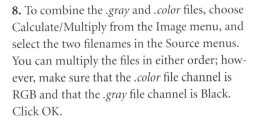

8. To combine the *.gray* and *.color* files, choose Calculate/Multiply from the Image menu, and select the two filenames in the Source menus. You can multiply the files in either order; however, make sure that the *.color* file channel is RGB and that the *.gray* file channel is Black. Click OK.

9. The Multiply command combines the values of the corresponding pixels in the two images. Areas that are black in the grayscale file remain black; areas that are white in the grayscale file become the color of the corresponding pixels of the RGB file. If you are satisfied with the result, save the file; otherwise, experiment with the Calculate commands for other effects.

Variation 1: Choose Difference in step 8 instead of Multiply. Make sure that the RGB file is Source 1 and the grayscale file is Source 2. Difference then subtracts the pixel values in Source 1 from the pixel values in Source 2. Areas that are white in both files remain white; areas that are black in either file become the color of the corresponding pixels in the other file.

Variation 2: Choose Add in step 8 instead of Multiply. To darken the new file, use a Scale value greater than 2; to darken the file even more, enter a negative value in the Offset field. To lighten the file, enter a positive value in the Offset field. In this example we used a Scale of 2 and an Offset of 0. See pages 72–77 for more information on Add, Scale, and Offset.

Variation 3: Choose Subtract in step 8 instead of Multiply. Subtract works like the Difference command except that you can enter a Scale and an Offset value as with the Add command. In this example, we used a Scale value of 2 and an Offset value of 128.

Variation 4: Choose Composite in step 8 instead of Multiply, and combine the two images with a third image. In this example, Source 1 was the RGB file, the Mask was the grayscale file, and Source 2 was the file that resulted from using Difference in *Variation 1*.

Creating different paint textures

Software needed: Adobe Photoshop 2.5

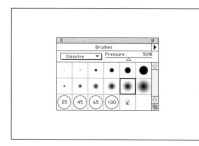

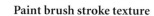

Paint brush stroke texture

1. First you will create a custom paint brush. Open a small grayscale file. Click the airbrush tool in the toolbox, and select a medium-sized to small soft brush from the Brushes palette. Set the mode to Dissolve.

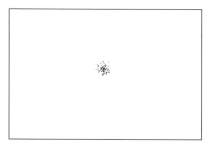

2. Select black as the foreground color. Click once with the airbrush tool (don't drag). This paint stroke will become your custom brush. Because you will use this brush with the smudge tool, it's important to keep the brush size small. Using a large brush with the smudge tool can significantly slow performance.

3. Click the rectangular marquee tool in the toolbox. Drag a marquee around the brush mark to select it.

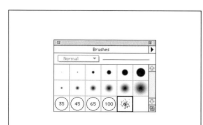

4. Choose Define Brush from the Brushes palette menu. The new brush appears in the Brushes palette.

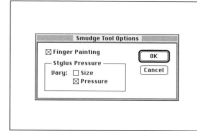

5. Now double-click the smudge tool in the toolbox. Select the Finger Painting option, and click OK.

6. Open the file in which you want to paint. Choose Show Colors from the Window menu, and select a foreground color in the Colors palette.

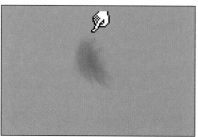

7. Begin painting. The Finger Painting option smudges the background texture and adds a bit of foreground color at the beginning of each stroke. To smooth out the texture and spread the color around, cross back over the first part of the stroke.

8. Keep in mind that while you are painting with the Finger Painting option, you are smudging the colors underneath the brush. Depending on the background color, you can end up with a very soft, impressionistic image.

9. If you want to change the colors in the image when you have finished, try increasing the contrast using Curves (⌘M) or Levels (⌘L). In this example, we opened Curves and clicked the Auto button to automatically adjust the contrast.

Marker pen effect

1. Select the paint brush tool. Choose Load Brushes from the Brushes palette menu, and load the *Drop Shadow Brushes* file from the Brushes & Patterns folder. Select a square-shaped brush, and set the mode to Multiply. Multiply combines the background colors with the painting color and darkens the effect. Set the opacity to 60%.

2. Open the file you want to paint, choose a color from the Colors palette, and begin painting. (Note that Multiply mode does not work with 100% white or 100% black paint.)

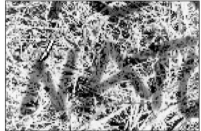

3. To darken the color, paint over an area more than once.

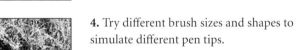

4. Try different brush sizes and shapes to simulate different pen tips.

Variation: Try using this technique to paint on a white background. You won't see the transparent effect until the strokes overlap.

Bleached effect

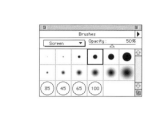

1. Select the paint brush tool. Select a brush from the Brushes palette, and set the mode to Screen. Screen combines the background colors with the painting color and creates a screened back, or bleached, effect. Set the opacity to 50%.

2. Open a color file, and choose a very light blue or violet as the foreground color. (Like Multiply, Screen mode does not work with 100% white or 100% black paint.) Begin painting. As your strokes overlap, the bleaching effect builds up.

Variation 1: To retain the gray values but remove the color, set the mode in the Brushes palette to Saturation. In Saturation mode, painting with white removes the color and leaves behind a grayscale version of the image.

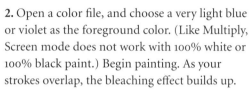

Variation 2: To change the color while retaining the shading, set the mode in the Brushes palette to Hue. Adjust the opacity. If you want to erase all existing color and replace it with a new color, use an opacity of 100%. Select a foreground color.

Begin painting. Photoshop replaces the hue values of the pixels and leaves the saturation and brightness values unaltered.

Enhancing clip art

Software needed: Adobe Photoshop 2.5

Many of the clip art books available to graphic designers and illustrators contain wonderful old woodcuts and engravings that you can customize for your artwork. This technique shows how to add color to a scanned woodcut in Adobe Photoshop while maintaining the original texture. To do this, you first trace the shapes in the woodcut and fill them with colors or blends; you then paste an inverted copy of the original woodcut on top of the shapes and fill the copy with one or more colors to create the texture.

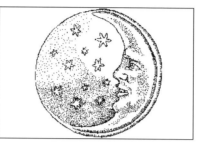

1. Scan the image at a larger size than you need, and save the original scan. Saving a larger copy of the image gives you the option of resizing and resampling the image for different situations. Scan the image at 1½ to 2 times the resolution you want for the final artwork. (If you don't plan to resize the image, skip to step 4.)

2. If the image isn't already a bitmap, choose Bitmap from the Mode menu to convert the image. For this type of image, resampling and resizing in Bitmap mode retains the clarity of the lines and prevents fuzziness. You can use different bitmap conversion options for different effects: we used the default options.

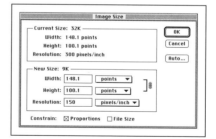

3. Choose Image Size from the Image menu and resize the image to the dimensions and resolution you want.

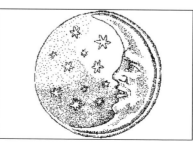

4. Now convert the image to Grayscale mode. Converting to grayscale allows you to copy the image into a channel in the next step.

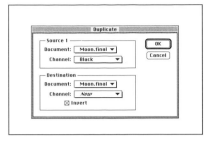

5. Choose Calculate/Duplicate from the Image menu. Source 1 should be the black channel of your grayscale file; the Destination should be a new channel of the same file. Select Invert to create a negative of the image, and click OK.

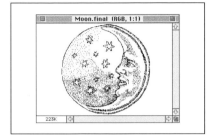

6. Convert the image to RGB mode. Because the original image has been saved in a separate channel (now channel #4), you can use the composite RGB channel to create your filled shapes—you'll then delete the original image from the RGB channel.

7. Open the Paths palette, and use the pen tool to trace the first shape in the woodcut. Because you'll eventually paste the original woodcut texture on top of the filled shapes, it's important to trace within the edges. When you've finished tracing the shape, save the path and name it after the shape so that you can keep track of the different paths.

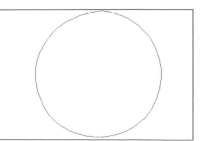

8. After saving the path, deselect it by clicking the checkmark next to its name. Then start the next path. If the image contains several shapes that will be filled with the same color, save them as one path. In this illustration, for example, all the stars were drawn and saved as one path.

9. Once you've finished tracing the image, select the entire image (⌘A), and delete it from the RGB channel. Select the path of the first shape you want to fill. If the shapes overlap, choose the backmost shape first.

10. From the Paths palette, choose Make Selection. Because the edges of the shape will be covered up by the woodcut texture, a 1-pixel feather is sufficient. Click OK.

11. Open the Colors palette, and select a foreground and background color for a gradient fill. Use the gradient fill tool to fill the selection.

12. When you are satisfied with the fill, deselect the path (⌘D). Click the next path listed in the Paths palette, and repeat steps 9–11 until all the paths are filled with a gradient fill or a color.

13. Choose Load Selection from the Select menu to load the original woodcut from channel #4 on top of the filled shapes. Choose a contrasting color from the Colors palette, and fill the selection (Option-Delete). To better view the results while experimenting with different fill colors, choose Hide Edges from the Select menu (⌘H).

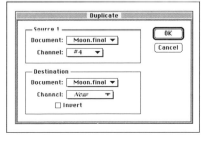

Enhancement: You can save portions of the original woodcut in different channels so that you can load and fill the final textures individually. To do this, follow steps 1 through 12; then choose Calculate/Duplicate from the Image menu to duplicate the woodcut selection channel you created in step 5. Copy channel #4 into a new channel of the same file (channel #5).

Select a part of the texture that you want to fill with one color. In this example, we selected the moon. (Note that the marquee shown in this illustration has been slightly enhanced for clarity.)

☙ *Adjusting Curves to generate a mask*
Often the building blocks you need to create a selection mask are in one of the existing color channels in the image. Determine which channel contains the most contrast in the area that you want to select. In this example, we chose the blue channel because we wanted to create a selection mask for the ocean.

Choose Inverse from the Select menu. Choose black as the foreground color, and fill the selection with black (Option-Delete).

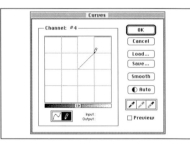

Choose Calculate/Duplicate from the Image menu and duplicate the channel into a new channel of the same image. Then choose Adjust/Curves from the Image menu. Click the eyedropper icon in the dialog box, and position the eyedropper over the area of the image that you want to make a mask of; note where on the Curves grid the circle indicator falls.

Now you'll subtract this new channel from the original channel and place the difference into a third channel. From the Image menu, choose Calculate/Difference. Select channel #4 as Source 1 and channel #5 as Source 2. The Destination should be a new channel of the same file (channel #6). Click OK.

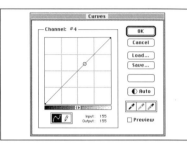

Click the pencil icon in the Curves dialog box. Use the pencil to draw a curve across the area of the grid you identified in the previous step. By adjusting the pixel values, you can create a precise selection of the area you want to isolate. Keep redrawing the curve until the selection is as you want it.

Channels #5 and #6 now each contain a portion of the original woodcut. If you wish to use more than two colors, repeat the preceding three steps until you have saved each color area in a separate channel. Return to the RGB channel (⌘0), and load selection #5. Fill the selection using Hide Edges (⌘H) to preview the results. When you are satisfied, deselect (⌘D).

After making adjustments, click the Smooth button at least once to soften any abrupt transitions in the mask. The smoother the mask, the better the results. Click OK. You now have the outline of your mask. Remember that selection masks act like negatives and that any gray areas will create a semitransparent mask.

Continue loading and filling selections until the texture is complete. (In this example, we filled the moon texture with green and the remaining texture with yellow.) When the artwork is as you want it, delete the unused channels to keep the file size to a minimum.

If necessary, adjust the contrast to make any gray values black. In this example, we used Levels (⌘L) to adjust the contrast, and then inverted the channel so that the ocean would be the selected area. We then removed some extraneous pixels from the ocean area. The result is a semitransparent mask of the ocean.

3 Text Effects

Photos masked by type

Software needed: Adobe Illustrator 3.0, Adobe Photoshop 2.0

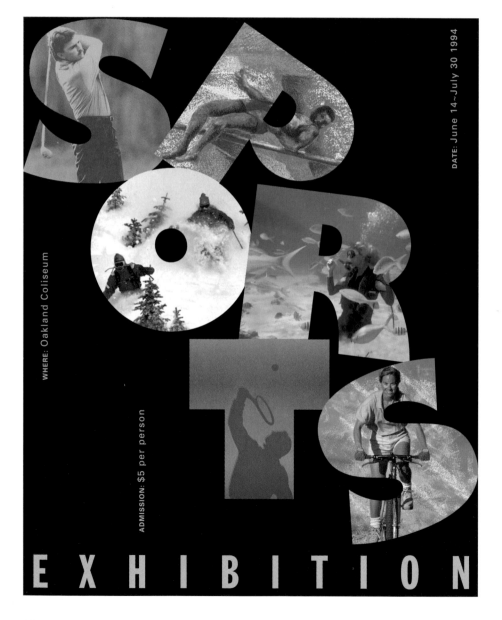

WHERE: Oakland Coliseum

ADMISSION: $5 per person

DATE: June 14~July 30 1994

You can create type masks for photographs in Adobe Photoshop or in Adobe Illustrator. Type masks in Photoshop are a little easier to create and print than in Illustrator. However, because Photoshop generates bitmapped type while Illustrator generates PostScript language outlines, you'll need to decide whether you want the anti-aliased edges of Photoshop's bitmaps or the smooth edges of Illustrator's outlines. Compare the results of the two methods in this procedure and decide which style you prefer. With both methods, heavy sans serif type-faces usually make a better mask. In addition, it's a good idea to scan the Photoshop file that you're masking at a higher resolution and size than you need in the final artwork. This will enable you to reposition and resize the photograph inside the type mask as needed.

Adobe Photoshop method

1. Open the Adobe Photoshop file in which you want to create the type mask. Choose New Channel from the Channels palette, and name the channel *type mask*. Create the type using the type tool, or use the Place command to place type from Adobe Illustrator into the channel.

2. Deselect the type (⌘D), and choose Map/Invert from the Image menu (⌘I) to invert the channel.

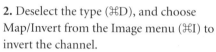

3. Return to the composite image channel, and choose Load Selection/*type mask* from the Select menu.

4. Open the Photoshop file that you want to mask with the type. Use the rectangular selection tool to select the area that you want to show through the type. Copy it to the Clipboard.

5. Return to the Photoshop file containing the active type mask selection, and choose Paste Into from the Edit menu. The photograph is now the floating selection. Drag the photograph into the position you want; then deselect it.

Adobe Illustrator method

1. Open the Adobe Illustrator file in which you want to create the type mask. Use the type tool to create the type. Use only a few letters to avoid printer memory problems.

2. Select the measure tool, and measure the height and width of the type. Write down these measurements for use in step 4.

3. Now switch to Adobe Photoshop, and open the file you want to mask with type.

4. Because you scanned the Photoshop image at a larger size and resolution than you will print it, you now need to crop the file. Double-click the cropping tool. Enter a height and width slightly larger than the measurements you wrote down in step 2. The resolution should be about twice the line screen (lpi) used to print the image.

5. Select the area of the photograph that you want to mask through the type. When you are ready to crop, click the scissors icon inside the cropping marquee.

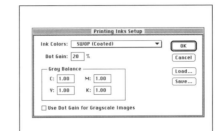

6. Next you need to convert the photograph to a CMYK file. From the File menu, choose Preferences/Printing Inks Setup. If you plan to print the file using standard U.S. four-color process, choose SWOP. If you plan to print only comps to a color printer, choose the printer type. Click OK. Then choose CMYK Color from the Mode menu to convert the file.

7. Use the Save As command to save the file. Select EPS as the format. If you want to see a color preview of the file in Illustrator, select the 8-bit preview option. Click OK.

8. Return to the Illustrator file. Choose Place Art from the File menu, and select the EPS file you just created. Choose Send to Back from the Arrange menu (⌘–) to place the image behind the mask. If you're using Adobe Illustrator 3.0 or 4.0, the image must be in front of the mask; in this case, choose Bring to Front from the Edit menu (⌘=).

9. Now select both the EPS image and the type, and choose Masks/Make from the Object menu. If you're using Adobe Illustrator 3.0 or 4.0, select only the type, and click the Mask option in the Paint Style dialog box. You can reposition the EPS file by deselecting it and then selecting only the EPS image and moving it around within the mask.

Three-dimensional type blocks

Software needed: Adobe Illustrator 3.0, Adobe Dimensions 1.0

You can use Adobe Dimensions to easily create three-dimensional type from type created in Adobe Illustrator. The effect you get depends on the typeface you use, the amount you extrude it in Dimensions, and the view and perspective you choose. All capital letters usually give the best results. Refer to the examples on this page to help determine the values to use as you go through this technique. Keep in mind that Dimensions shades the three-dimensional artwork by adding black; therefore, you'll need to choose a fill color light enough to show the shading. You can also select the faces of the three-dimensional letters after they've been exported to Illustrator, and then stroke or paint the faces in Illustrator.

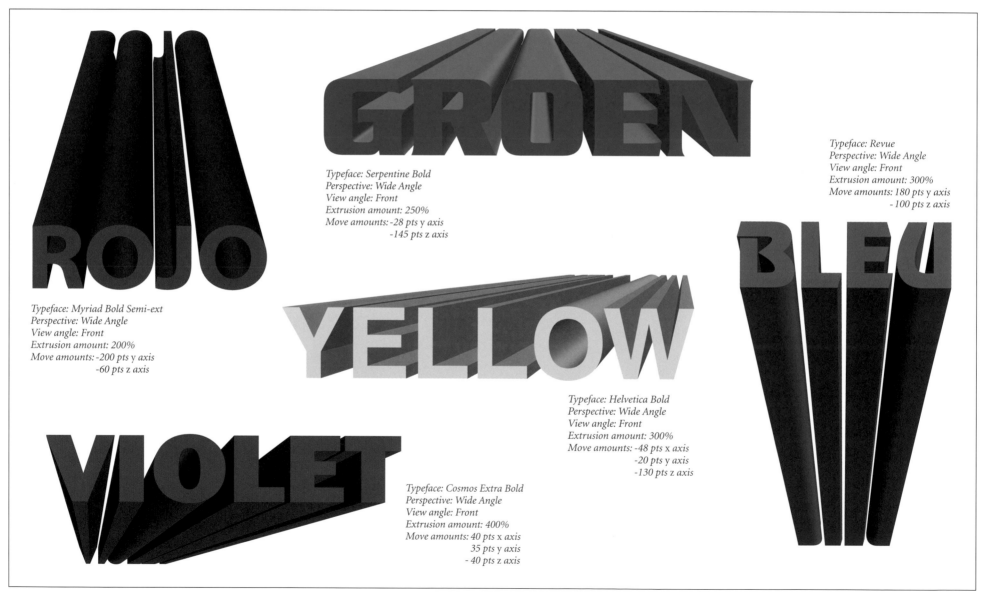

Typeface: Serpentine Bold
Perspective: Wide Angle
View angle: Front
Extrusion amount: 250%
Move amounts: -28 pts y axis
-145 pts z axis

Typeface: Revue
Perspective: Wide Angle
View angle: Front
Extrusion amount: 300%
Move amounts: 180 pts y axis
-100 pts z axis

Typeface: Myriad Bold Semi-ext
Perspective: Wide Angle
View angle: Front
Extrusion amount: 200%
Move amounts: -200 pts y axis
-60 pts z axis

Typeface: Helvetica Bold
Perspective: Wide Angle
View angle: Front
Extrusion amount: 300%
Move amounts: -48 pts x axis
-20 pts y axis
-130 pts z axis

Typeface: Cosmos Extra Bold
Perspective: Wide Angle
View angle: Front
Extrusion amount: 400%
Move amounts: 40 pts x axis
35 pts y axis
- 40 pts z axis

1. Create a word or headline in Adobe Illustrator. A bold sans serif typeface works best with this technique. Adjust the letter and word spacing. Leave enough space between the letters so that the sides of the letters will be distinguishable when extruded. Paint the type with the desired fill.

6. Using the selection tool, click the dotted bounding box around the type. Choose Extrude from the Operations menu (⌘-Shift-E). In this example, we used a Relative Depth of 300%. Refer to the sample artwork on the facing page to determine the Relative Depth amount for your letterforms. Click OK.

2. Make sure that the type is as you want it. (Once you convert the type to outlines, making changes is much more difficult.) Using the selection tool, click the baseline of the type to select the type.

7. Now you will use the Move dialog box to adjust the view. With the type selected, choose Move from the Operations menu. Make sure that the Absolute option is selected. Click Clear and then click Apply to center your artwork at 0,0,0. To view the letters from above, enter a negative *y*-axis value; to view them from below, enter a positive value.

3. Choose Create Outlines from the Type menu. Save the file and name it *Type.ai*. (If you are using Adobe Illustrator 5.0, you can copy the outlines to the Clipboard and then paste them into Dimensions instead of importing the file.)

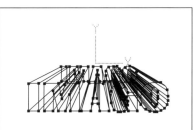

8. Adjust the *z*-axis value to change the depth perspective. Enter a positive number to make the artwork appear to recede; use a negative number to make the artwork appear to come forward. Click Apply.

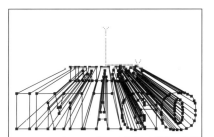

4. In Adobe Dimensions, import the file called *Type.ai*. By default, Dimensions displays the artwork with a perspective of None and a view angle of Off-axis Front.

9. In the Preferences dialog box (⌘K), enter a Draft Blends value between 15 and 25; then choose Draft Render from the View menu (⌘Y). The higher number of blends in the draft will enable you to make lighting decisions.

5. Change the view angle to Front (⌘1) and the perspective to Wide Angle. You are now ready to add dimension to your type.

10. Adjust the Lighting (⌘L) and Surface Properties (⌘I). In this example we placed a light at the upper left and right of the artwork at 100% intensity and one light directly behind the artwork at 21% intensity. Use the guidelines on pages 14–17 to determine the correct number of blends for the final shaded render. Then choose Shaded Render (⌘-Shift-Y).

Creating three-dimensional metallic type

Software needed: Adobe Illustrator 5.0, Adobe Dimensions 1.0

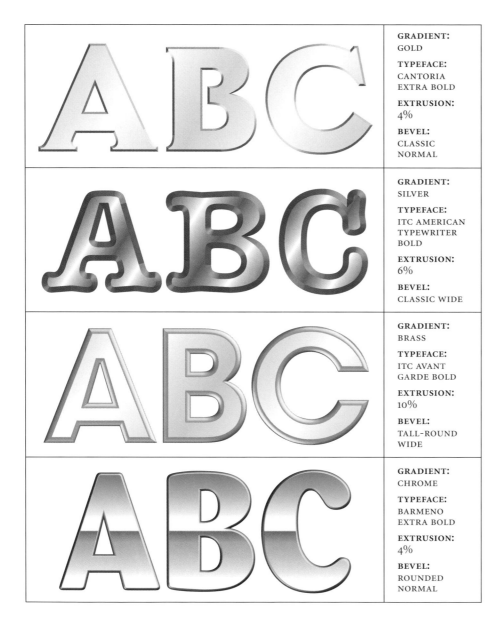

GRADIENT:	GOLD
TYPEFACE:	CANTORIA EXTRA BOLD
EXTRUSION:	4%
BEVEL:	CLASSIC NORMAL

GRADIENT:	SILVER
TYPEFACE:	ITC AMERICAN TYPEWRITER BOLD
EXTRUSION:	6%
BEVEL:	CLASSIC WIDE

GRADIENT:	BRASS
TYPEFACE:	ITC AVANT GARDE BOLD
EXTRUSION:	10%
BEVEL:	TALL-ROUND WIDE

GRADIENT:	CHROME
TYPEFACE:	BARMENO EXTRA BOLD
EXTRUSION:	4%
BEVEL:	ROUNDED NORMAL

1. Create the type you want using Adobe Illustrator. Allow enough space between the letters for beveled sides in the metallic characters. Click the selection tool in the toolbox, and select the type.

2. From the Type menu, choose Create Outlines.

3. Paint the letters with a medium blue for a steely look. (We used a mix of 100% cyan and 50% magenta.) See the sample artwork on the facing page for examples of other metallic effects. Fill the letters with a flat color only. The fill will serve as a base color for the beveled edges in Adobe Dimensions. Save the file with the filename suffix *.2–D*.

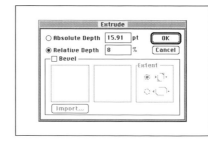

4. Switch to Dimensions and import the *.2–D* Illustrator file (⌘-Shift-I). Change the view angle to Front (⌘1). The perspective should be None. Make sure that the type is selected.

5. From the Operations menu, choose Extrude (⌘-Shift-E). Choose Relative Depth and enter an extrusion amount. Refer to the sample artwork for help determining the best extrusion amount for the typeface you are using. In this example, we used a Relative Depth extrusion of 8%. Do not click OK.

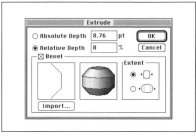

6. Select the Bevel option in the Extrude dialog box. Click Import to import a bevel design from the Bevel Library folder; then click OK. (If a message appears telling you that the edges of your artwork will intersect, click No, and then select a different bevel or reduce the extrusion amount.)

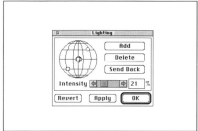

7. Choose Draft Render (⌘Y) to preview the beveled edges. If you aren't satisfied with the effect, return to Artwork mode (⌘W), undo the extrusion (⌘Z), and try again with different values.

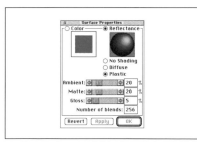

8. Use the Lighting dialog box (⌘L) to create high-contrast shadows that will enhance the metallic look. In this example, we placed three lights in front of the type: one in the center, one at the lower left, and one at the upper right. We lowered the intensity of the two side lights to 21%.

9. To create a shiny, hard surface, choose Surface Properties (⌘I). Select Reflectance and then Plastic. Change the Matte percentage to about 20% and the Gloss percentage to 5%. Then enter the correct number of blends for your artwork using the guidelines on pages 14–17.

10. Choose Shaded Render from the View menu (⌘-Shift-Y). Save the file as a Dimensions file with a suffix of *.dim*. Export it (⌘-Shift-S) as an Illustrator file with a suffix of *.ai 3–D*.

11. In Adobe Illustrator, open the *.ai 3–D* file. With the direct-selection tool, click the face of the first letter. Hold down the Shift key and select the other faces and their counterforms (for example, the inside shapes of the *O* and *P*). Do not select the beveled edges of the letters.

12. Use the Import Styles command to import the *Metal Gradients* file from the Adobe Illustrator Gradients & Patterns folder. Open the Paint Style palette (⌘I), and apply the Steel Blue gradient fill to the letters. The fill is applied to each letter in the selection. Choose Hide Edges from the View menu (⌘-Shift-H) so that you can better view the results.

13. Type an angle of about 30° in the Paint Style palette, and click Apply. To apply the gradient fill across all the letters continuously, open the Info palette and use the gradient fill tool to draw a 30° line from the top left of the letters to the bottom right.

14. Experiment with other angles until you have the effect you want. When you are satisfied with the results, use Save As to save the file as an Adobe Illustrator 5.0 file.

Wraparound initial caps

Software needed: Adobe Illustrator 3.0

1. Select the type tool, and drag to draw a rectangular area to contain a body of text. Choose Import Text from the File menu, and open a text file to import the type into the rectangular shape.

2. Click the type tool anywhere in the text block, and choose Select All from the Edit menu (⌘A). If necessary, change the typeface and leading.

3. Click the rectangle tool in the toolbox. This selects the text box and text baselines. Position the pointer directly over the upper left corner of the text box, and drag until the new box covers the area in which you want the large initial cap.

4. Paint the new rectangle with no fill and no stroke.

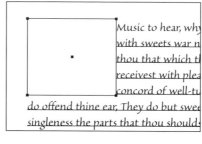

5. Use the selection tool to select both the text block and the new unpainted rectangle. Choose Make Wrap from the Type menu. You now have a space for a large initial cap.

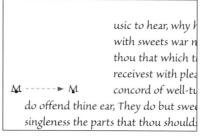

6. Select the type tool, select the first letter of the type, and cut it to the Clipboard (⌘X). Then click the type tool in the toolbox to deactivate the text block. Click outside the text block, and paste the letter from the Clipboard (⌘V). For easier positioning change the alignment to Centered (⌘-Shift-C). Move the initial cap to the lower center of the blank wrap area.

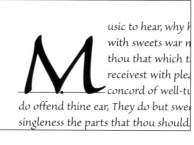

7. Change the point size to the desired width or height. Be sure to leave space around the cap so that the type and the cap don't touch.

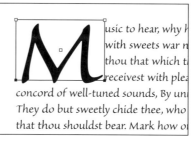

8. Adjust the position of the letter to align with the top and side of the text block. Use the direct-selection tool to select the bottom two anchor points of the invisible wrap box, and adjust the space to fit the initial cap better; then select the side two anchor points of the box and adjust them as needed.

9. Deselect to view the results.

Type on a circular path

Software needed: Adobe Illustrator 3.0

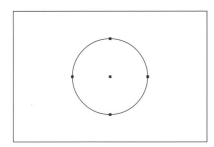

1. Select the oval tool, and create a circle that defines the inside baseline of your type. Select a type style and size.

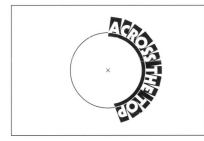

2. Switch to Artwork view so that you can better see the relationship of the type to the circle. Click the path-type tool, and click the top anchor point of the circle. Type what you want to appear along the top of the circle. All caps work better than lowercase letters because no ascenders or descenders bisect the arc that the letters form.

3. With the I-beam still visible at the end of the type you just created, choose Select All from the Edit menu (⌘A). From the Type menu, choose Alignment/Centered (⌘-Shift-C).

4. Click the selection tool in the toolbox to select the circle and the type. Position the pointer on the I-beam at the center of the text, and begin to drag around the outside of the circle; then hold down the Option key to copy the type. When you reach the circle's bottom anchor point, release the mouse button and then the Option key.

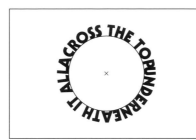

5. Click the path-type tool and select the newly created block of type. (Don't worry if it overlaps the top copy; you will adjust the point size later.) Replace the type with the type that you want to appear along the bottom of the circle.

6. Click the selection tool in the toolbox. Drag a marquee around the center point of the circle to select the upper and lower type and the circle. Change the point size using the Type Style dialog box or the keyboard shortcuts. (Press ⌘-Shift-> to increase the point size; press ⌘-Shift-< to decrease the point size.)

7. Deselect everything, and click just the lower type. Position the pointer on the I-beam and drag upwards to flip the type to the inside of the circle. (You can also double-click the I-beam to flip the type.)

8. While the lower type is still selected, choose Character from the Type menu (⌘T), and enter a negative number for the Baseline Shift, or use the keyboard shortcut (Option-Shift-Down Arrow) to move the type down until the tops of the letters touch the outer edge of the circle. Preview the results.

9. Now add a border. With the circle selected, select the oval tool, and begin dragging from the circle's center point. Hold down the Option and Shift keys to draw the oval from its center and constrain it to a circle. Release the mouse button and then the Option and Shift keys. Repeat this step to create an outer border; then send the border to the back (⌘-).

Creating a gradation with type

Software needed: Adobe Illustrator 3.2, Any Adobe multiple master typeface

You can make a large block of text visually appealing by creating a subtle gradation in the typeface's weight or width, or both. You can use this technique with an entire text block, or to selectively alter pull quotes, excerpts, or captions. To achieve a smooth gradation in type, you need to use an Adobe multiple master typeface; other typefaces don't contain enough weights and widths. This technique creates a gradation in the typeface's weight. For a different effect, try varying the width, or both the weight and width. Note that if you create a gradation using both the weight and width, you must create more typeface instances. In this case, set up a grid with the weight values along the vertical axis and the width values along the horizontal axis.

Take gigantic surfaces, conceived as infinite, cloak them in color, shift them menacingly and vault their smooth **pudency. Shatter and embroil finite parts and bend d**rilling parts of the void infinitely together. Paste smoothing **surfaces over one another. Wire lines movement, real m**ovement rises real tow-rope of a wire mesh. Flaming lines, **creeping lines, surfacing lines. Make lines fight together** and caress one another in generous tenderness. Let points **burst like stars among them, dance a whirling round, a**nd realize each other to form a line. Bend the lines, crack **and smash angles, choking revolving around a point. I**n waves of whirling storm let a line rush by, tangible in **wire. Roll globes whirling air they touch one another. I**nterpermeating surfaces seep away. Crates corners up, straight and crooked and **strangled crates b**oxes. Make lines pulling sketch a net ultramarining. Nets embrace compres**s Antony's torment. Make nets firewave and run off into lines, thicken into surfaces. Net the **nets. Make veils blow, soft folds fall, make cotton drip & water** gush. Hurl up air soft and w**hite through 22-thousand candle power arc lamps. Take** wheels and axles, hurl them **up and make them sing mighty creation of aquatic giants.** Axles dance midwheel roll gl**obes barrel. Cogs flair teeth, find a sewing machine that** yawns. Turning upward or bo**wed down the sewing machine beheads itself, feet up.** Take a dentist's drill, a meat gri**nder, a car-track scraper, take buses & pleasure cars, bicycles, tandems & their tires, also war-time ers**atz tires and deform them. Take lights and deform them as brutally as** you can. Make locomotives c**rash into one another, curtains and portières make threads of spider** webs dance with window frames and break whimp**ering glass. Explode steam boilers to make** railroad mist. Take petticoats and other kindred arti**cles, shoes and false hair, also ice skates and** throw them into place where they belong, and alway**s at the right time. For all I care, take man-traps, automatic pistols, infernal machines, the tinfish and the funnel, all of course in an artistically deformed condition. Inner tubes are highly** recommended. Take in short everything from **the hairnet of the high class lady to the propelle**r of the S.S. Leviathan, always bearing in mind **the dimensions required by the work. Even peo**ple can be used. People can even be tied to back-**drops. People can even appear actively, even in** their everyday position, they can speak on two legs, **even in sensible sentences. Now begin to wed your materials**. For example, you marry the oil **cloth table cover t**o the home owner's loan a**ssociation, you bring the l**amp cleaner into a relationship **with the marriage** between Anna Blume & A-**natural, concert pitch. You** give the globe to the surface to **gobble up and yo**u cause a cracked angle to **be destroyed by the beam** of a 22-thousand candle power **arc lamp. You mak**e a human walk on his (he**r) hands and wear a hat on** his (her) feet, like Anna Blume. **A splashing of foa**m. Now begins the fire of **musical saturation. Organs** backstage sing and say: "Futt, **futt." The sewing** machine rattles along in **the lead. A man in the wings says: 'Bah.' An-other suddenly e**nters and says: 'I am st**upid.' (all rights reserved.) Between them a clergyman kneels** upside down and cries o**ut and prays in a loud voice: 'Oh mercy seeth and swarm disint**egration of amazement **Halleluia boy, marry drop of water.' A water pipe drips with un**inhibited monotony. A **stream of ice cold water runs down the back**

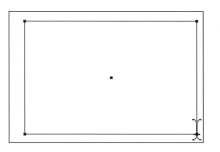

Good sense is, of all things among men, the most equally distributed; forever one thinks himself so abundantly provided with it, that those even who are the most difficult to satisfy in everything else, do not usually desire a larger measure of this quality than they already possess. And enthuse it is not likely that all are mistaken the conviction is rather to beheld as testifying that the power of judging aright and of distinguishing truth from error, which is properly what is called good sense or reason, is by nature equal in all men; and that the diversity of

Good sense is, of all things among men, the most equally distributed; forever one thinks himself so abundantly provided with it, that those even who are the most difficult to satisfy in everything else, do not usually desire a larger measure of this quality than they already possess. And enthuse it is not likely that all are mistaken the conviction is rather to beheld as testifying that the power of judging aright and of distinguishing truth from error, which is properly what is called good sense or reason, is by nature equal in all men; and that the diversity of our opinions, consequently, does not arise from some being endowed with a larger share of reason than others, but solely from this, that we conduct our thoughts along different ways, and do not fix our attention on the same objects. For to be possessed of a vigorous mind

Weight of beginning line	•830 / 300 •	Width of beginning line
# of lines in the gradation		
Weight of ending line	•215 / 300 •	Width of ending line

1. Open an Adobe Illustrator file. Select the type tool, and drag to create a text block large enough for the type you will modify.

2. Choose Import Text from the File menu to enter the type. Make sure that the alignment is set to Justify (⌘-Shift-J).

3. With the type tool, click anywhere inside the text block. Choose Select All from the Edit menu (⌘A). Select a multiple master typeface with the style, size, and width that you want. In this example, we used one of the primary fonts included with the Myriad™ multiple master typeface. Adjust the word spacing and kerning.

4. You now need to determine the intermediate weights that will give you a smooth gradation. To do this using a formula, create a chart like the one shown here. To do this automatically using Adobe Illustrator, go on to step 6.

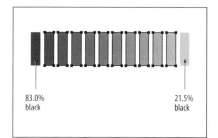

Weight of beginning line →830/300
774/300
718/300
662/300
606/300
550/300
Weight & width of instances needed 495/300
439/300
383/300
327/300
271/300
Weight of ending line →215/300

Width of beginning line

Width of ending line

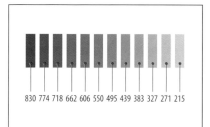

83.0% black   21.5% black

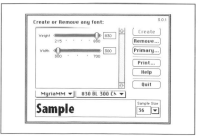

830 774 718 662 606 550 495 439 383 327 271 215

Create or Remove any font: 3.0.1
Weight 215 ————●—— 830 830
Width 300 ——●———— 700 300
Create
Remove...
Primary...
Print...
Help
Quit
MyriaMM ▾ 830 BL 300 CN ▾
Sample Sample Size 36 ▾

5. Calculate the increment for increasing the typeface weight using the following formula: **(Largest value – Smallest value)/(# lines – 1)** Add the result to the smallest weight and then to each subsequent weight in the gradation. In our example: $[(830–215) = 615]/[(12–1)= 11]=56$; therefore, we added 56 to each step (line) in our gradation ($56+215=271$; $271+56=327$, etc.).

6. As an alternative to steps 5 and 6, you can calculate the intermediate weights in Adobe Illustrator. Create a small rectangle, and paint it with a percentage of black that is 10% of the heaviest typeface weight in your gradation. Create another rectangle using 10% of the lightest typeface weight. In our example, we used 10% of 830 and 215: 83% and 21.5%.

7. Now select both rectangles, and click the blend tool in the toolbox. Click the corresponding points of each rectangle to display the Blend dialog box. Enter the number of steps between the beginning and ending lines of your type gradation. (In our example, we entered 10 because we had a total of 12 steps.) Click OK.

8. Use the direct-selection tool to select each rectangle; record the black value from the Paint Style palette. Multiply each value by 10. You now have the intermediate weights needed to create a smooth type gradation.

9. Open the Font Creator utility located in your Multiple Masters folder. Select the typeface and the weight you want for the beginning line. Click Create to create the typeface.

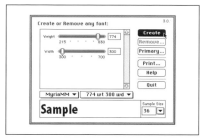

Create or Remove any font: 3.0
Weight 215 ————●—— 830 774
Width 300 ——●———— 700 300
Create
Remove...
Primary...
Print...
Help
Quit
MyriaMM ▾ 774 wt 300 wd ▾
Sample Sample Size 36 ▾

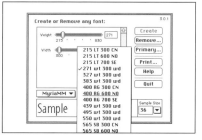

Create or Remove any font: 3.0.1
Weight 215 ——●———— 830 271
Width 300 ——●———— 700
Create
Remove...
Primary...
Print...
Help
Quit
215 LT 300 CN
215 LT 600 NO
215 LT 700 SE
✓271 wt 300 wd
327 wt 300 wd
383 wt 300 wd
400 RG 300 CN
400 RG 600 NO
400 RG 700 SE
439 wt 300 wd
495 wt 300 wd
550 wt 300 wd
565 SB 300 CN
565 SB 600 NO
MyriaMM ▾
Sample Sample Size 36 ▾

Good sense is, of all things among men, the most equally distributed; forever one thinks himself so abundantly provided with it, that those even who are the most difficult to satisfy in everything else, do not usually desire a larger measure of this quality than they already possess. And enthuse it is not likely that all are mistaken the conviction is rather to beheld as testifying that the power of judging aright and of distinguishing truth from error, which is properly what is called good sense or reason, is by nature equal in all men; and that the diversity of our opinions, consequently, does not arise from some being endowed with a larger share of reason than others, but solely from this, that we conduct our thoughts along different ways, and do not fix our attention on the same objects. For to be possessed of a vigorous mind

Good sense is, of all things among men, the most equally distributed; forever one thinks himself so abundantly provided with it, that those even who are the most difficult to satisfy in everything else, do not usually desire a larger measure of this quality than they already possess. And enthuse it is not likely that all are mistaken the conviction is rather to beheld as testifying that the power of judging aright and of distinguishing truth from error, which is properly what is called good sense or reason, is by nature equal in all men; and that the diversity of our opinions, consequently, does not arise from some being endowed with a larger share of reason than others, but solely from this, that we conduct our thoughts along different ways, and do not fix our attention on the same objects. For to

Good sense is, of all things among men, the most equally distributed; forever one thinks himself so abundantly provided with it, that those even who are the most difficult to satisfy in everything else, do not usually desire a larger measure of this quality than they already possess. And enthuse it is not likely that all are mistaken the conviction is rather to beheld as testifying that the power of judging aright and of distinguishing truth from error, which is properly what is called good sense or reason, is by nature equal in all men; and that the diversity of our opinions, consequently, does not arise from some being endowed with a larger share of reason than others, but solely from this, that we conduct our thoughts along different ways, and do not fix our attention on the same

10. Enter the second weight you recorded in step 5 or step 8. Click Create.

11. Continue creating new instances of the typeface until you have a version for every weight in your chart. Then quit the Font Creator.

12. Return to your text file in Adobe Illustrator. You will select the lines of type and change the typeface into progressively lighter weights; the type will reflow each time. To avoid missing a word when it rerags the line, select the line you want to change and the one below it. Start by selecting the top two lines of the text.

13. Change the typeface to the beginning (heaviest) weight typeface in your blend. Don't worry about the extra lines and letters that were changed. The lines below will be changed in turn.

14. Now select the second and third lines of the text. Change the typeface to the second heaviest typeface in your blend. Continue to change each consecutive pair of lines in the text block until you reach the ending (lightest) typeface weight in your chart.

4 Special Effects

Creating frames and concentric borders

Software needed: Adobe Illustrator 5.0

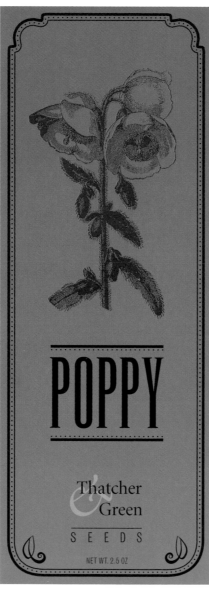

Creating evenly spaced concentric shapes requires more than simply scaling and copying the shapes. This technique shows how to use the new Offset Path filter in Adobe Illustrator 5.0 to create a frame or border with multiple, evenly spaced outlines. The offset amount you use with the Offset Path filter depends on the amount of space you want between the shapes and on the stroke values you're using. Use the formula at the beginning of this technique to determine what offset amount you need to get the results you want.

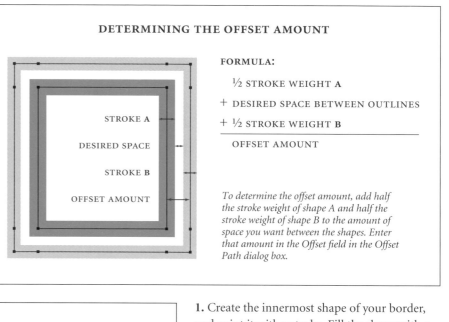

DETERMINING THE OFFSET AMOUNT

STROKE A

DESIRED SPACE

STROKE B

OFFSET AMOUNT

FORMULA:

$\frac{1}{2}$ STROKE WEIGHT **A**

+ DESIRED SPACE BETWEEN OUTLINES

+ $\frac{1}{2}$ STROKE WEIGHT **B**

_____

OFFSET AMOUNT

To determine the offset amount, add half the stroke weight of shape A and half the stroke weight of shape B to the amount of space you want between the shapes. Enter that amount in the Offset field in the Offset Path dialog box.

1. Create the innermost shape of your border, and paint it with a stroke. Fill the shape with a color if you want the space between your shapes to be filled. In this example, we left the shape unfilled.

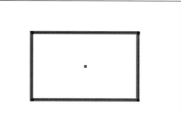

2. To create the next largest frame, select the shape, and choose Objects/Offset Path from Filter menu. Enter the offset amount (use the formula above), and click OK.

3. The filter expands all sides of the shape by the amount entered to create the offset shape. Choose Hide Edges from the View menu (⌘-Shift-H) to better view the results.

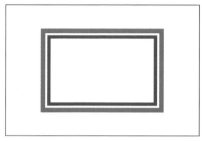

4. If desired, change the color or stroke of the new frame using the Paint Style palette (⌘I).

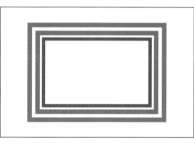

5. Make sure that the outer frame is still selected, and then reapply the filter. To use the same offset value, choose Offset Path from the top of the Filter menu (⌘-Shift-E). To reopen the Offset Path dialog box, hold down the Option key and choose Offset Path from the top of the menu.

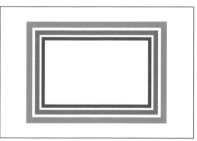

6. Adjust the color and stroke weight, if desired.

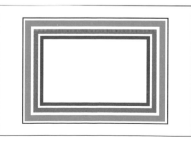

7. Repeat steps 4–6 to create as many frames as you need.

❧ *Stars and shapes with acute angles*

If your shape has very acute angles, the lines of the offset shape created by the Offset Path filter will intersect and create corners like those in this star:

To correct the overlapping corners, select the shape, and choose Pathfinder/Unite from the Filter menu. The Unite filter creates a single path from the outline of all selected objects, ignoring any paths within the outline.

❧ *Wrapping a graphic around an invisible shape*

You can create different effects with Adobe Illustrator artwork by mapping the artwork onto invisible shapes in Adobe Dimensions. First, create the three-dimensional shape, and map the graphic onto it using Artwork Mapping.

Now select the whole shape, and choose Surface Properties from the Appearance menu. Paint the object with no fill and no stroke, and click Apply. Before you create a Shaded Render view, be sure to select the Shade Mapped Artwork option in the Preferences dialog box.

Creating reverse shapes

Software needed: Adobe Illustrator 3.0

The effect of overlapping type and graphics is common in Art Deco graphic design. You can use these techniques, however, for any overlapping shapes whose colors you want to change at the point where the shapes overlap. If you want to be able to move the shapes after creating the reversed effect, use the Compound Path method. If you are using Adobe Illustrator 5.0 and you don't need to move the shapes after creating the effect, use the Filter method. The Filter method is the easier of the two methods and, unlike the Compound Path method, it allows you to select and paint shapes individually.

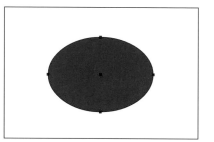

Compound Path method

1. Create the background element of your design, and paint it. Keep in mind that the paint attributes of this object will be adopted by the other objects in the compound path.

2. Create or paste the other objects into the artwork, and position them as you want them in the final design.

3. If you are using type as an element of the design, you must create outlines before you can make a compound path. With the selection tool, select the baseline of the text object; then choose Create Outlines from the Type menu. If you're using Adobe Illustrator 3.0 or 4.0, choose Bring to Front from the Edit menu to make the object the frontmost object in the artwork.

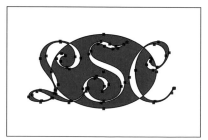

4. Now select all objects, and choose Compound Paths/Make from the Object menu (⌘8). (With Adobe Illustrator 3.0 or 4.0, choose Make Compound from the Paint menu.)

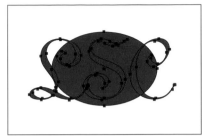

5. You may find that some objects are solid that you wanted transparent or vice versa. To correct this problem, you must reverse the direction of these paths. Deselect everything (⌘-Option-A), and use the direct-selection tool to select the path that you want to change. If you don't have this problem, skip to step 7.

6. Choose Attributes from the Object menu (⌘-Control-A), and click the Reverse Path Direction option. (With Adobe Illustrator 3.0 or 4.0, this option is in the Paint Style dialog box.)

7. Deselect everything, and check your work.

8. To adjust elements of the compound path, use the direct-selection tool to select and move the elements. Remember that any object placed behind a transparent shape in the artwork will show through the shape.

Filter method (Adobe Illustrator 5.0 only)
1. Create the background element of your design. It's not necessary to paint the object: when you apply the filter, the object will take on the paint attributes of the frontmost object in the selection.

2. Create or paste the other objects into the artwork and position them as you want them in the final design. Keep in mind that the paint attributes of the frontmost object will be adopted by the other objects after you use the filter.

3. If you are using type as an element of the design, you must create outlines before you can make a compound path. With the selection tool, select the baseline of the text object; then choose Create Outlines from the Type menu.

4. Now select all objects in the artwork, and choose Pathfinder/Exclude from the Filter menu. Deselect everything (⌘-Shift-A), and check your work. The Exclude filter knocks out any overlapping areas of color between the objects.

5. Because each remaining area of color is now a separate object, you can no longer move the original artwork elements. You can, however, change the colors of the objects—something you can't do with the Compound Path method. Use the direct-selection tool to select the objects that you want to change.

Variation: To create separate shapes from the overlapping areas instead of knocking them out, use the Divide Fill filter. You can then fill each shape with a different color.

Blending images together

Software needed: Adobe Photoshop 2.5

This technique shows you how to blend two images together in such a way that one fades out as the other fades in. While the example here illustrates an even fade at the 50% mark of a linear blend, you can create different effects by choosing other fade points or by using a radial blend. You can use this technique to blend selections in images, entire images, or the backgrounds of images. If you are blending an entire image or background, skip the instructions that refer to loading a selection.

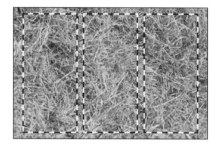

1. Open a file in which you will blend your images. If you want to create the fade in a selected area, select that area and choose Save Selection from the Select menu to create a new channel. In the Channels palette, double-click the new channel and name it *blend area*. In this example, we wanted the fade to occur in three rectangular areas.

2. Choose New Channel from the Channels palette. Name the channel according to the selection's position in the blend. For example, if you plan to make the images fade from top to bottom and this is the upper image, name the channel *top*; if they will fade from left to right, name the channel *left*. Click OK.

3. Double-click the gradient fill tool in the toolbox, and select the type of blend you want. Set the midpoint skew to the point at which you want the second image to begin fading into the first. In this example, we used a linear blend and a midpoint skew of 50% to create an even fade between the images. Click OK.

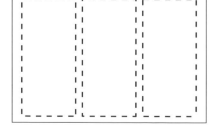

4. Click the default colors icon in the toolbox to set the foreground and background colors to black and white. If you're blending your images inside a selection, choose Load Selection from the Select menu and load the *blend area* selection you created in step 1. If not, continue with step 5.

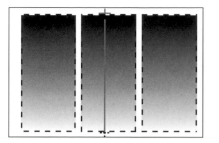

5. Now you will make a blend in your *top* selection channel to create a mask for the fading effect. Position the gradient fill tool at the top of the selection, hold down the Shift key, and drag to the bottom of the selection. (If you are creating a fade from left to right, hold down the Shift key, and drag from the left to the right side of the selection.)

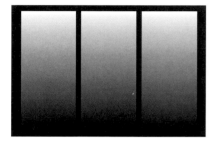

6. Deselect (⌘D) and choose Map/Invert from the Image menu (⌘I) to invert the channel. You now have a mask for the top image that fades from opaque at the bottom (100% black) to transparent at the top (100% white).

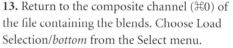

7. Next you will create an inverse of this mask for the bottom image. From the Image menu, choose Calculate/Duplicate. Source 1 should be the *top* channel of your current document; the Destination should be a new channel of the same document. Double-click the new channel in the Channels palette, and name the channel *bottom*.

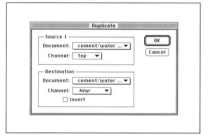

8. The *bottom* channel should now be the active window. If you saved a selection in step 1, choose Load Selection/*blend area* from the Select menu. Invert the blend by choosing Map/Invert from the Image menu (⌘I). You now have a mask for your bottom image that fades from opaque at the top (100% black) to transparent at the bottom (100% white).

9. You are now ready to blend the two images. Open the files that contain the images to be blended. These files should have the same resolution as your final file; if they don't, pasting the images will change their dimensions. Select the image that will be at the top of the blend. If possible, select an area slightly larger than you need. Copy the selection to the Clipboard.

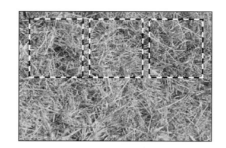

10. Return to the composite channel (⌘0) of the file you opened in step 1. From the Select menu, choose Load Selection/*top*. Don't be confused when you load a selection that has a gradation in it. Although the entire blend is selected, Adobe Photoshop only shows what is from 0% to 50% black as selected.

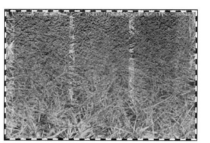

11. Choose Paste Into from the Edit menu to paste the image that you copied to the Clipboard in step 9 into the blend area. If necessary, drag the image while it is still selected to reposition it within the blend area.

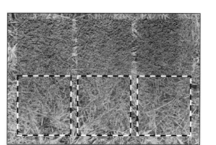

12. Now select the image that will be at the bottom of the blend, and copy it to the Clipboard.

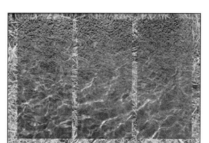

13. Return to the composite channel (⌘0) of the file containing the blends. Choose Load Selection/*bottom* from the Select menu.

14. Choose Paste Into from the Edit menu. If necessary, drag the selection to reposition it within the blend area. Deselect (⌘D), and save the file.

Creating vignettes

Software needed: Adobe Photoshop 2.5

It's easy to create a vignette in Adobe Photoshop. Until you paste the vignette into place, however, it's hard to see the effect of the feathered edges. You can use Photoshop's Quick Mask mode to create vignettes and to experiment freely with different feathering amounts without affecting the original image.

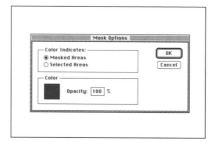

1. Open the Adobe Photoshop file containing the color or grayscale image that you want to vignette. Double-click the Quick Mask icon, and change the opacity of the mask to 100%. If you are using an image that contains a lot of red, change the mask color to a color that's easily distinguishable from the colors in the image.

2. Use any of the selection tools to select the part of the image that you want to vignette. Keep in mind that the feathered edges of the selection will extend on both sides of the selection marquee.

3. To adjust the position of the selection marquee, simply place the pointer inside the marquee and drag to the new position. Because you are in Quick Mask mode, the image itself is not affected by the move.

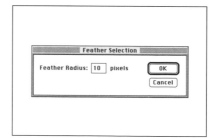

4. Choose Feather from the Select menu. Enter a Feather Radius, and click OK. (In this example, we used a radius of 10 pixels.) The effect of a given Feather Radius varies with the size of the selection, the resolution of the file, and the image itself.

5. Choose Inverse from the Select menu to select everything outside the vignette.

6. Fill the new selection (Option-Delete) to create the mask.

7. Deselect everything (⌘D) to preview the vignette. If you need to redraw the shape or change the amount of feathering, double-click the eraser tool to delete the mask, return to step 2, and try again. In this example, we redrew the selection to make the vignette larger.

8. Now click the Standard mode icon in the toolbox to turn the mask into a selection. Copy the selection to the Clipboard.

9. Open the file into which you are going to paste the vignette. If you plan to place the vignette in another program, open a new file. Paste the vignette. Pasting positions the vignette in the center of the window. Reposition the vignette if desired; then deselect it, and save the file.

❧ *Quick Mask design overlay*

When working with type or graphics on top of a photograph, it's sometimes difficult to reposition the graphics without altering the underlying image. Quick Mask mode in Adobe Photoshop 2.5 provides a quick, memory-efficient way to modify artwork on top of a Photoshop image.

When creating opaque masks in Quick Mask mode, make sure that the foreground color is black. If the foreground color is anything but black, any new masks you create in Quick Mask mode will be semitransparent.

Open the image on which you want to work, and click the Quick Mask mode icon at the bottom of the toolbox. Because nothing was selected when you switched to Quick Mask mode, clicking the Quick Mask icon does not affect the screen display. Now add the type or graphics you want from Adobe Illustrator. The graphics will appear a light, transparent red—the default mask color. If the color is not easily distinguishable from the underlying image, double-click the Quick Mask icon, double-click the color box in the Mask Options dialog box, and use the Color Picker to select a new overlay color.

You can use Quick Mask mode to add type and graphics to the mask layer and to easily move, scale, and rotate the graphics on top of the image. When the design is as you want it, switch back to Standard mode to fill the selection with blends, solid colors, or other images.

Using scanned objects as masks

Software needed: Adobe Photoshop 2.5

At times, you may want to use as a mask a photograph or an image that cannot be easily drawn on the computer. For example, you can create a mask from a leaf, a handprint, a cloth texture, or a hand-drawn or painted form. If you have a flatbed scanner, you can scan almost anything that isn't wet. This technique shows how to use a scanned image as a mask to frame or contain another image. To create the final artwork, you use three files: the mask, the background image, and the image to be masked. To avoid unexpected results, all the files should be the same resolution.

1. Scan the object or artwork from which you want to create the mask. Don't bother scanning it as a color file because it will be a grayscale image in the selection mask channel. Save the scan as a grayscale Adobe Photoshop file.

2. Open the file, and select the area of the scan that you want to use as the mask. Copy the selection to the Clipboard.

3. Open the file that will be the background for the masked image. For the best results, the background image should be lighter than the image to be masked. A lighter background helps the mask edges show up better.

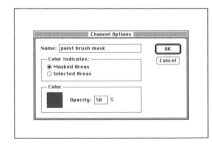

4. Now you will create a new channel for the mask. Choose New Channel from the Channels palette menu. Name the channel *paint brush mask*. Click OK.

5. Paste the mask that you copied to the Clipboard in step 2 into the new channel.

6. Deselect the mask (⌘D), and choose Map/Invert from the Image menu (⌘I).

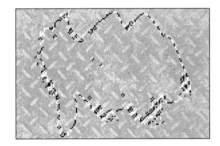

7. To see where the mask is positioned on your background image, return to the composite image channel (⌘0), and choose Load Selection from the Select menu. If you don't need to reposition the mask, skip to step 9.

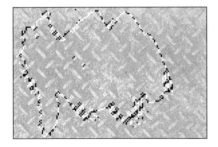

8. To reposition the mask, hold down the Command and Option keys, and drag the selection. When the selection is positioned as you want it, release the mouse button, and then the Command and Option keys. To save the repositioned mask, choose Save Selection from the Select menu.

9. Open the file containing the image that you want to mask.

10. Using the rectangular marquee tool, select an area slightly larger than the mask. Copy the selection to the Clipboard.

11. Return to the background image file. The mask selection should still be active. Choose Paste Into from the Edit menu.

12. With the pasted selection still active, drag to adjust its position within the mask. Deselect, and save the new image.

Variation: You can adjust the opacity of the pasted image so that some texture from the background image shows through the mask. Before you deselect in step 12, choose Composite Controls from the Edit menu, and set the opacity to less than 100%. In this example, we used 60%.

Filter combinations

Software needed: Adobe Illustrator 5.0

The new plug-in filters in Adobe Illustrator 5.0 enable you to quickly produce effects that in the past would have required hours of exacting studio work. For example, the Pathfinder™ filters let you quickly select, divide, and merge objects based on their paths, strokes, and fills. The techniques in this section are intended to give you a starting point for working with filters; don't hestitate to change the filter values or to apply a filter more than once to get the effect you want. To reapply a filter using the same filter values, press ⌘-Shift-E. To reopen the dialog box of the last used filter, hold down the Option key, and choose the filter name from the top of the Filter menu.

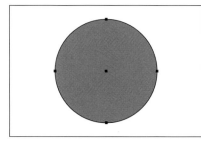

Scalloped seals

1. Use the oval tool and the Shift key to draw a circle.

Three-dimensional stars

1. Choose Create/Star from the Filter menu and change the Points value to 4. (We used the default Radius values of 20 and 50.)

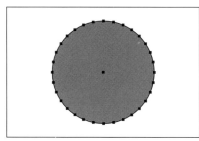

2. Choose Objects/Add Anchor Points from the Filter menu. The number of times you apply the filter depends on the size of the circle; the distance between the anchor points determines the size of the scallops. We applied the filter three times.

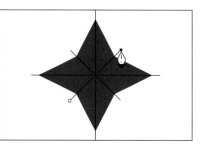

2. Select the pen tool and draw horizontal, vertical, and diagonal lines across the star between the anchor points.

3. Choose Stylize/Punk from the Filter menu. In this example, we used a value of 5%.

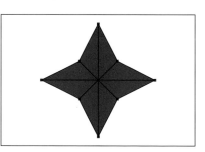

3. Select the star and the lines, and choose Pathfinder/Divide Fill from the Filter menu.

Variation: For an inverse effect, apply the Bloat filter in step 3 instead of the Punk filter. This example shows a Bloat filter value of 5%.

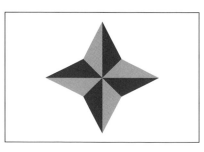

4. Use the direct-selection tool to select the shapes, and fill them with an alternating highlight and shadow color.

Twirled stars

1. Choose Create/Star from the Filter menu. We drew a five-pointed star using the default Radius values of 20 and 50. (You can preview different effects in the Star dialog box by changing the number of points and the two Radius values and then clicking the Points text box.)

2. Choose Objects/Add Anchor Points from the Filter menu. Depending on the size of the star, you may want to apply the filter more than once. (We applied it two times.) The number of anchor points you add determines the smoothness of the curves in the final shape.

3. Choose Distort/Twirl from the Filter menu. In this example, we twirled the filter 90°. Use the rotate tool to rotate the star if desired.

Variation 1: You can vary the effect by changing the number of anchor points and the Twirl angle. In this example, we applied the Add Anchor Points filter once and then applied the Twirl filter using an angle of 60°.

Variation 2: You can also achieve different effects using different types of stars. Here we created a nine-point star, applied the Add Anchor Points filter three times, and then applied the Twirl filter using an angle of 100°.

Color palettes

1. Save a PICT file that contains colors you want to use as an Adobe Illustrator palette. You can create a color palette from an Adobe Photoshop file or from any other file saved in PICT format.

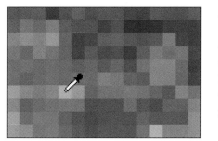

2. Choose Create/Mosaic from the Filter menu, and open the PICT file. (If your computer runs out of memory, try choosing a smaller number of tiles or applying the filter to a selection in the PICT file.) Deselect everything (⌘-Shift-A). Use the eyedropper tool to select any color from the mosaic.

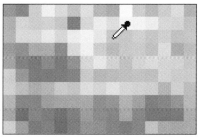

Variation: After applying the Mosaic filter, try using different Colors filters to modify the mosaic. In this example, we used the Adjust Colors filter to decrease the black by 100%.

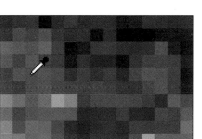

In this example, we applied the Saturate filter after applying the Mosaic filter. You can apply the filter any number of times for different effects.

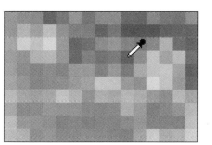

You can also apply the Desaturate filter to get a palette with subtle differences between the colors. Experiment with different filters and filter values.

Tissue paper backgrounds
1. Save a PICT file that contains the colors you want in the background.

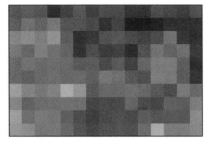

2. Choose Create/Mosaic from the Filter menu, and open the PICT file at the desired size. (If your computer runs out of memory, try choosing a smaller number of tiles or applying the filter to a selection in the PICT file.) Choose Hide Edges from the View menu to better view the results.

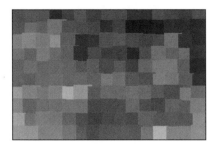

3. Choose Objects/Scale Each from the Filter menu, and scale the mosaic tiles using the Random option. In this example, we entered 150% in the Horizontal and Vertical text boxes. Using the Random option then scales the tiles randomly from 0 to 150%.

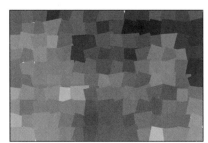

4. Choose Objects/Rotate Each from the Filter menu, and rotate the mosaic tiles using the Random option. In this example, we rotated the tiles 40°.

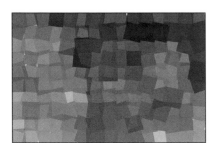

5. Choose Pathfinder/Mix Hard from the Filter menu to mix the overlapping colors and create a transparent effect.

Antiqued type
1. Create the type you want, and with the type selected, choose Create Outlines from the Type menu. (Because the paths created with this technique may be quite complex, you may need to antique a few letters at a time.)

2. Choose Objects/Add Anchor Points from the Filter menu. Depending on the size of your type, you may want to apply this filter more than once. The anchor points must be very close together to give the right effect in step 3.

3. Choose Distort/Tweak from the Filter menu, and enter the same value in the Horizontal and Vertical text boxes. Use a very low value. (We used 0.4 points). Click OK.

4. Choose Objects/Rotate Each from the Filter menu, and rotate the letters slightly using the Random option. In this example, we rotated the letters 6°.

5. Choose Objects/Move Each from the Filter menu, and move the letters slightly using the Random option. In this example, we used a Horizontal value of 1 point and a Vertical value of 0.4 points. Experiment with different values until the effect is as you want it.

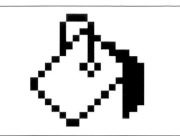

Bitmap graphics

1. Save a bitmap PICT file in Adobe Photoshop or in another application.

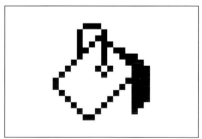

2. Choose Create/Mosaic from the Filter menu, and select the PICT file. In the Mosaic Filter dialog box, make sure that the Current Size Width equals the Number of Tiles Width. Select the Lock Width option, and click Use Ratio. These steps ensure that the number of tiles in the mosaic equals the number of points in the bitmap. Deselect the mosaic (⌘-Shift-A).

3. Select a background tile, and then choose Select/Same Paint Style from the Filter menu to select all tiles of the same color.

4. Press Delete to delete the background tiles.

5. Select the tiles that you want to define as one shape, and choose Pathfinder/Unite from the Filter menu. Paint or edit the new object as desired.

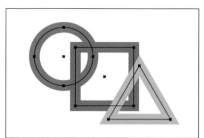

Interlocking stroked objects

1. Create the stroked objects that you want to link.

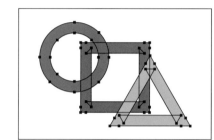

2. Make sure that the objects are selected, and choose Objects/Outline Stroked Path from the Filter menu. Applying the Outline Stroked Path filter defines each stroked path as an object.

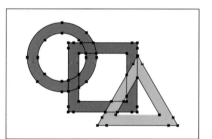

3. To delete the extra corner points created by the filter, select each object with corners and choose Pathfinder/Unite from the Filter menu. Then select all objects, and choose Pathfinder/Divide Fill. Applying the Divide Fill filter defines the overlapping color areas as separate objects.

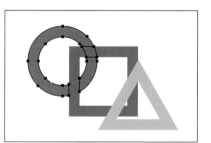

4. Determine which objects should be behind other objects to create the interlocking effect. Use the direct-selection tool to select the objects that you want to fill with one color. Then choose Pathfinder/Unite from the Filter menu to combine those objects. (Note that selected objects take on the paint attributes of the topmost object when the Unite filter is applied.)

5. Adjust the fill and stroke attributes of the new objects as desired.

Creating silhouette masks

Software needed: Adobe Photoshop 2.5

One of the more difficult tasks in working with photographs, including digital photographs, is to mask out the human face and figure. The difficulty lies in trying to separate the fine texture of hair and the smoothness of skin from the background. The easiest way to do this is to shoot the subject against a blue screen and use the "Composite Photographs" technique described in Design Essentials. Many times, however, you need to use existing photographs and can't shoot against a blue screen. This section describes different techniques for creating silhouette masks based on the color of the background you are masking and the color of the background you want in the final artwork.

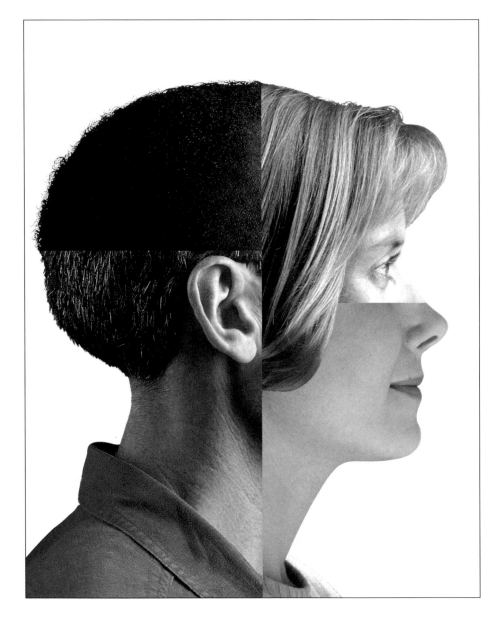

Subject against a flat, light background; to be pasted onto a dark background

1. Open an RGB file with a subject against a light background.

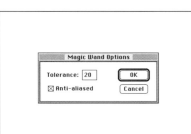

2. Double-click the magic wand tool in the toolbox. Make sure that the Anti-aliased option is selected, and set the tolerance between 10 and 32.

3. Position the magic wand tool on the background, and click. If areas of the background remain unselected, hold down the Shift key and click those areas to add them to the selection.

4. Choose Inverse from the Select menu. You now have a rough selection of your subject.

5. Some areas in the hair, eyelashes, moustache, and so on, will probably need touching up. The easiest way to touch up a selection is to use Quick Mask mode. Quick Mask mode enables you to see the image while you work on the mask. Click the Quick Mask mode icon in the toolbox.

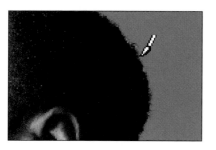

6. Select the paint brush tool in the toolbox. Select a small, soft brush from the Brushes palette. Paint with the brush to add areas to the mask that the magic wand tool missed. To remove areas from the mask, change the foreground color to white, and remove them with the brush.

7. Once you have cleaned up the mask, make it a selection by clicking the Standard mode icon in the toolbox. Choose Save Selection from the Select menu, and then copy the selection to the Clipboard.

8. Open the file into which you will paste the silhouette.

9. Paste the silhouette onto the background and move it into position. Do not deselect it.

10. Choose Hide Edges from the Select menu (⌘H) so that you can better evaluate how well the silhouette blends in with the background. Some light pixels around the edge of the figure may need to be removed.

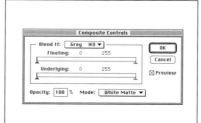

11. The easiest way to remove light edge pixels is to use a white matte. Choose Composite Controls from the Edit menu, and choose White Matte from the Mode menu. Click OK. Depending on the background and edge colors, applying the white matte may completely remove the light edges. If any light edges remain, continue to step 12.

12. A slower but more precise way to clean up the edge pixels and blend them into the background is to use the Clone option of the rubber stamp tool. First, choose Inverse from the Select menu to select the background of the silhouette.

13. Choose Hide Edges to better view the edge of the figure. Double-click the rubber stamp tool, and select the Clone (aligned) option. Select a small, soft brush from the Brushes palette. Position the pointer slightly more than a brush width from the edge that needs retouching, hold down the Option key, and click to sample the background color.

14. Drag with the rubber stamp tool to clone the background into the areas that need retouching. You may need to sample the background several times as the angle of the silhouette edges change. When you have finished, deselect the silhouette, and save the file.

Subject against a flat, dark background; to be pasted onto a white background
1. Open an RGB file with a subject against a dark background.

2. Follow steps 2 through 9 of the preceding method. When you have pasted the selection onto the white background, choose Hide Edges (⌘H) to better view the edge of the silhouette. Some dark pixels around the edges of the figure will probably need to be removed.

3. First try to fix this problem using a black matte. Choose Composite Controls from the Edit menu. Choose Black Matte from the Mode menu. Depending on the background and edge colors, applying the black matte may completely remove the dark edges. If any dark edges remain, continue to step 4.

4. Choose Inverse from the Select menu to select the background of the silhouette.

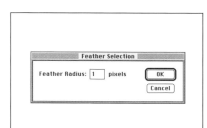

5. To remove the remaining dark pixels, you need to enlarge the selection slightly. Choose Feather from the Select menu, and enter an amount of 1 pixel. Click OK.

6. Choose Hide Edges to better view the edge of the silhouette. Select a small brush from the Brushes palette, and change the foreground color to white. Begin painting around the edge of the silhouette to remove the unwanted dark pixels.

7. Continue painting until all dark edges have been removed. Then deselect the image, and save it.

Subject against a mixed-color or textured background; to be pasted onto another mixed background
1. Open an RGB file with a subject against a mixed background.

2. Follow steps 2 through 9 of the first method. You will probably need to use both the magic wand tool and the lasso tool to create the rough selection. Be sure to select the Anti-aliased option with both tools.

3. Open the file into which you will paste the silhouette. Make sure that this file and the RGB subject file have the same file size and resolution. Choose Take Snapshot from the Edit menu to place a copy of the background in an image buffer. You will use the image in step 8 for touch-up.

4. Paste the silhouette onto the background, and move it into position. Do not deselect it.

5. To soften the selection edges slightly, choose Feather from the Select menu, and enter an amount of 1 pixel. Click OK.

6. Choose Inverse from the Select menu to select the background of the silhouette.

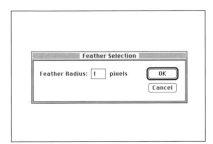

7. Choose Hide Edges from the Select menu (⌘H) so that you can better evaluate how well the silhouette blends in with the background. Some pixels around the edge of the figure may need to be removed.

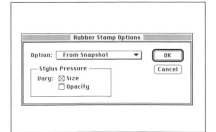

8. Double-click the rubber stamp tool in the toolbox. Choose From Snapshot from the Option menu. Click OK.

9. Begin painting around the edges of the figure. The feathered edge of the selection helps make a smooth transition between the background and the pasted silhouette.

10. If you need to touch up some pixels masked by the selection, deselect everything, and then carefully paint the pixels using a soft, very small brush and a lower opacity.

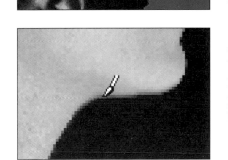

Variation 1: When pasting a silhouette onto a flat-color background, try using the paint brush tool to touch up the edges of the figure. As in the preceding methods, feather the edges of the pasted selection by 1 pixel. Then choose Inverse from the Select menu. Hide the selection edges and touch up the edge pixels using the same color as the background.

Variation 2: When pasting a silhouette onto a dark background, use the method described in Variation 1, but choose the Darken mode in the Brushes palette. Darken mode ensures that only pixels lighter than the painting color are affected by the paint brush.

Using the Calculate feature in Adobe Photoshop

Software needed: Adobe Photoshop 2.0

The Calculate feature in Adobe Photoshop is one of Photoshop's most powerful and at the same time most often overlooked tools. The concept of calculating pixel values between channels can be confusing for artists who don't easily see the correlation between the traditional world of overlays, film, and printing plates and the digital-imaging world of channels. This section explains the concepts most important to understanding the Calculate feature and provides examples of the different Calculate commands. For additional examples of using the Calculate commands, see "Painting and Calculating" on pages 34–35.

While the Calculate feature in Adobe Photoshop may seem unintuitive to many artists, many Calculate commands do in fact enable you to mimic techniques used in traditional photography and printing for combining images. The Calculate/Multiply command, for example, is designed to give the same results as superimposing two positive transparencies on a light table; the Calculate/Screen command produces the same effect as superimposing two film negatives and printing the result on photographic paper. (Note that these two commands are also modes in Photoshop's Brushes palette and in the Composite Controls dialog box.)

Two concepts are fundamental to understanding the Calculate feature. The first is that every pixel is assigned a value from 0 (off, or black) to 255 (on, or white). The second is that Calculate works by overlaying the pixels in two or more channels. For this reason, any files you calculate between must have exactly the same size and resolution. If you're unable to select the files you want in one of the Calculate dialog boxes, double-check the size of the files by holding down the Option key and selecting the file size box in the bottom left corner of the window.

When working with composite images, it's also important to understand that Adobe Photoshop calculates the pixel values in *each set* of color channels and then combines them in a single channel. If you're just learning to use the Calculate feature, it's easier to experiment with grayscale files or single channels of color images.

Two Calculate commands, Constant and Duplicate, stand out from the others in that they operate on a single image only. Constant (not illustrated in this section) simply lets you fill a channel with a brightness value that you specify. Duplicate provides a useful way of creating an unsaved copy of an image or channel. Using Duplicate is faster and requires less memory than copying an image to the Clipboard and pasting it into a new file.

ORIGINAL

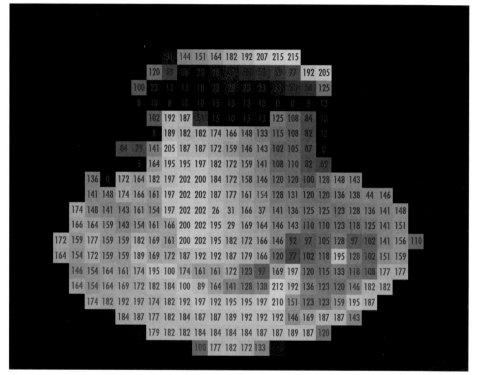

What are pixel values? *Every Photoshop channel is made of pixels. Each pixel is assigned a value based on its brightness level in RGB mode. The values range from 0 to 255, where 0 indicates a pixel that is off, or 100% black, and 255 indicates a pixel at maximum brightness. When translating pixel values into C, M, Y, or K percentages, keep in mind that a pixel value of 0 (black) equals a color value of 100%; a pixel value of 255 (white) equals a color value of 0%. This difference is based on the fact that in the world of monitors and display devices, the absence of color results in black; while in the world of printing, the absence of color results in white. If you find this confusing, open the Info palette and move the pointer around the image to compare the RGB pixel values with the CMYK percentages. You can also use the chart on the facing page to translate pixel values into percentages and vice versa.*

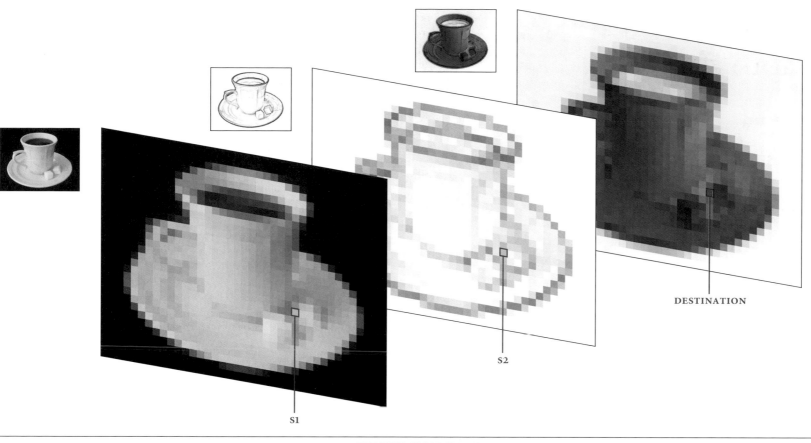

Calculate works by overlaying pixels. *When you choose the Calculate/Add command, Photoshop adds the value of each pixel in Source 1 (S1) to the value of each corresponding pixel in Source 2 (A2). The sums are placed in the corresponding pixels of a new file, called the Destination. Each file must contain exactly the same number of pixels across and down for the Calculate commands to work. If the files' dimensions or resolutions are different, you won't be able to select the files in the Calculate dialog box. If this happens, use Image Size or the cropping tool to resize the files, and then try again.*

DESTINATION

S2

S1

PERCENT COLOR TRANSLATED TO PIXEL VALUE

PERCENT COLOR	PIXEL VALUE	PERCENT COLOR	PIXEL VALUE	PERCENT COLOR	PIXEL VALUE	PERCENT COLOR	PIXEL VALUE	PERCENT COLOR	PIXEL VALUE	PERCENT COLOR	PIXEL VALUE	PERCENT COLOR	PIXEL VALUE	PERCENT COLOR	PIXEL VALUE	PERCENT COLOR	PIXEL VALUE	PERCENT COLOR	PIXEL VALUE
100	0	90	26	80	51	70	77	60	102	50	128	40	154	30	179	20	205	10	230
99	3	89	28	79	54	69	79	59	105	49	131	39	156	29	182	19	207	9	233
98	5	88	31	78	56	68	82	58	108	48	133	38	159	28	184	18	210	8	236
97	8	87	33	77	59	67	84	57	110	47	136	37	161	27	187	17	212	7	238
96	10	86	36	76	61	66	87	56	113	46	138	36	164	26	189	16	215	6	241
95	13	85	38	75	64	65	90	55	115	45	141	35	166	25	192	15	218	5	243
94	15	84	41	74	67	64	92	54	118	44	143	34	169	24	195	14	220	4	246
93	18	83	44	73	69	63	95	53	120	43	146	33	172	23	197	13	223	3	248
92	20	82	46	72	72	62	97	52	123	42	148	32	174	22	200	12	225	2	251
91	23	81	49	71	74	61	100	51	125	41	151	31	177	21	202	11	228	1	253
																		0	255

SOURCE 1		SOURCE 2		DESTINATION	

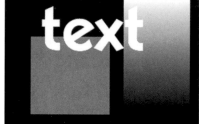

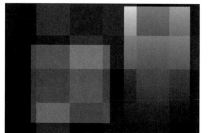

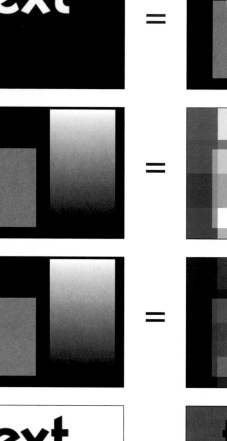

Add

Scale: 1; Offset: 0

The Add command's default settings simply add the pixel values in the two channels. This is a good way to easily combine nonoverlapping images in two channels.

Because higher pixel values represent lighter colors, adding channels with overlapping pixels results in lightening of the image. Black areas in both channels, however, remain black (0 + 0 = 0). White in either channel results in white (255 + any value = 255 or greater).

In this example, we used a Scale value of 2. Add divides the sum of the pixel values by the Scale amount and then adds the Offset value to the sum. Increasing the Scale value darkens the image. Entering a negative Offset value darkens the image further; entering a positive Offset value lightens the image.

Blend

Weight: 70%

Blend adds the pixel values in two channels and lets you assign a weight to the values for a transparent or double-exposure effect. Black areas in both channels remain black.

In this example, we used a weight of 70%. Blending the images then adds 70% of the color in each channel of Source 1 to 30% of the color in each channel of Source 2 (100% − 70% = 30%).

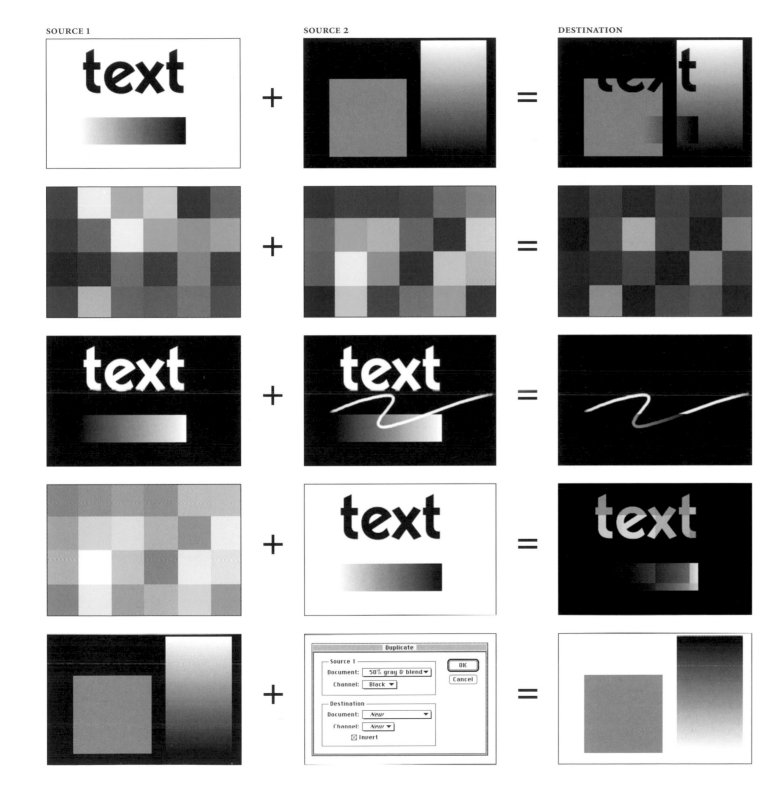

Darker

Darker compares the brightness values of the corresponding pixels and displays the darker of the two. With two single-channel files, such as these grayscale files, using Darker simply retains the darker values in both files.

With composite color images, Darker compares the brightness value in each set of color channels and then combines the darker values in one file. In this case, the colors in the resulting image may be very different from the colors in either source image.

Difference

Difference subtracts the pixel values in Source 2 from the pixel values in Source 1 and displays the result. Difference is a useful tool for dividing an image into components. See the Variations on pages 35 and 40 for examples of this technique.

Any black pixels in Source 2 become the value of the corresponding pixels in Source 1 (any value – 0 = any value). Any white pixels in Source 2 become black (any value – 255 = 0 or less).

Duplicate

Duplicate copies pixel values from one channel to another. Use Duplicate to experiment with an unsaved copy of an image or a mask. To create an inverted copy of a channel, click the Invert option in the Duplicate dialog box.

SOURCE 1   SOURCE 2   DESTINATION

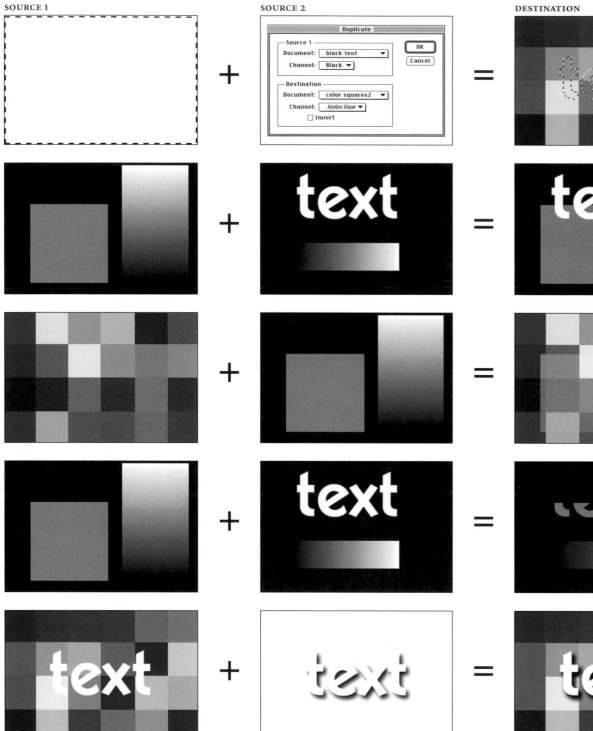

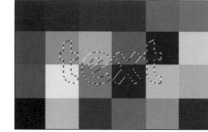

If you're working with a very large file, you can keep the file size to a minimum by saving your selection channels in a separate file. When you are ready to load the selection, use Duplicate and choose *Selection* as the Destination channel.

Lighter

Lighter compares the brightness values of the corresponding pixels and displays the lighter of the two. With two single-channel files, such as these grayscale files, using Lighter simply retains the lighter values in both files.

With composite color images, the Lighter command compares the brightness value in each set of color channels and then combines the lighter values in one file. In this case, the colors in the resulting image may be very different from the colors in either source image.

Multiply

The Multiply command multiplies the pixel values in the two files and divides the result by 255. The effect is analogous to superimposing two positive transparencies on a light table.

Black in either file results in a value of black (any value $\times\ 0 = 0$). White in either file results in the corresponding pixel value in the other file (($255 \times$ any value) $\div\ 255 =$ any value). In most cases, intermediate color and gray values in both files result in darker colors in the Destination file.

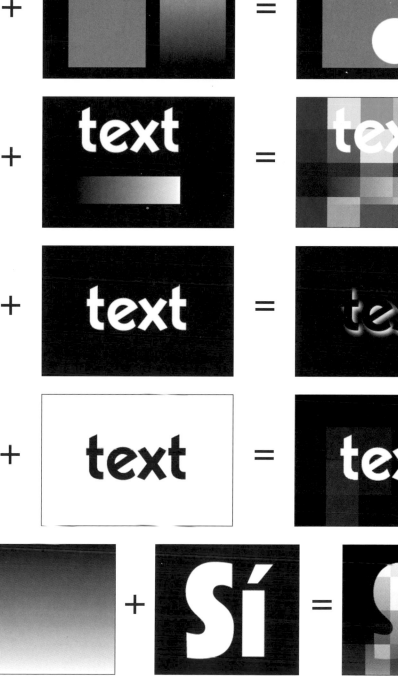

Screen

Screen produces the effect of superimposing two film negatives and printing the result on photographic paper. Screen is essentially the inverse of Multiply.

White in either file results in white. Black in either file results in the corresponding color in the other file. In most cases, intermediate color and gray values result in lighter colors in the Destination file.

Subtract

Like Difference, the Subtract command subtracts the pixel values in Source 2 from the pixels values in Source 1. As with the Add command, the result is then divided by a Scale value and added to an Offset value. You can use Scale and Offset values to lighten or darken the effect.

Increasing the Scale value darkens the result. Using a negative Offset value darkens the results further; using a positive Offset value lightens the result. In this example, we used an Offset value of 128.

Composite

Composite combines three images: a foreground image (Source 1), a background image (Source 2), and a mask. The images are then blended so that the foreground image is given more weight in the areas revealed through the mask, and the background image is given more weight in the area covered by the mask.

5 Creating Files for Video

Making custom masks for movies

Software needed: Adobe Photoshop 2.5 and Adobe Premiere 3.0

At times you may want to use an image or a specially shaped selection area as a mask in a movie. This technique shows how to create a mask in Adobe Photoshop and then use it in Adobe Premiere as an Image Matte through which another clip plays. You can use this technique with still images or with stationary parts of moving images. You can also use the Track Matte key type to create a moving mask. To ensure that the image mask registers perfectly with the image in the movie, make sure that the pixel width and height of the mask match the width and height of the movie.

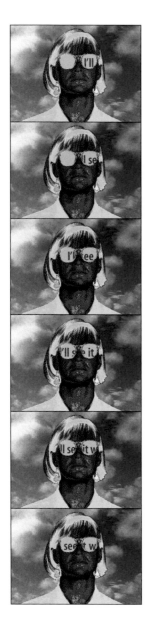

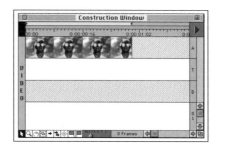

1. To create the mask in Adobe Photoshop, you must first open the image that you will use to create the mask. If you are masking a still image, simply open the image in Adobe Photoshop, and skip to step 5. If you are masking a moving image, start Adobe Premiere, and open the movie in which you want the mask.

2. Click the Frame Forward button to locate the frame in the movie that you want to use to create the mask.

3. Choose Export Frame as PICT from the File menu to save the frame as a PICT file.

4. Open the PICT file in Adobe Photoshop.

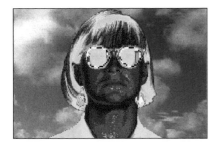

5. Use the selection tools to select the mask area. In this example, we used the pen tool to select the area in the sunglasses, and then chose Make Selection from the Paths palette menu.

6. Save the selection to a channel by choosing Save Selection/*New* from the Select menu. Do not save over channel #4. Deselect (⌘D), and then click the new channel in the Channels palette.

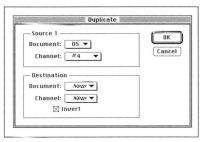

7. Now you will place the mask into a separate file. Choose Calculate/Duplicate from the Image menu. Duplicate the mask channel you just created into a new file.

8. Save the file with the suffix *.mask* in the folder with your other movie project files.

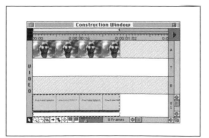

9. Open your Premiere movie project. Select the clip that will play through the mask and place it in the S1 channel. In our example, we selected a still-image clip containing type and applied Motion Settings to animate the type.

10. With the clip selected, choose Transparency from the Clip menu (⌘T). Choose Image Matte as the Key Type. Click the Choose button, and select the *.mask* file. Make sure that the background is visible by clicking the page peel icon under the Sample box. Then click OK.

11. To preview the effect, set the work area bar to the part of the movie that contains the mask, and press the Enter key. (If you are using Adobe Premiere 2.0, you must save the project before you can preview it.)

12. When you are satisfied with the effect, save the project, and make a movie (⌘K).

Modifying a filmstrip

Software needed: Adobe Premiere 3.0, Adobe Photoshop 2.5

Even though Adobe Premiere 3.0 includes many of the same features as Adobe Photoshop, such as filters and type, there are still times when you may want to modify a Premiere movie in Photoshop. For example, you may want to use Photoshop to paint on a filmstrip or to add a special effect to a selected area of a frame. To modify a movie in Photoshop, you create a filmstrip of your video clip in Premiere and then open it in Photoshop. If you want to modify several consecutive frames, you apply the change to each frame.

1. In Adobe Premiere, open the clip that you want to alter.

2. Choose Export/Filmstrip from the File menu. Premiere automatically names the file with the suffix *.film*. Select the frame rate that you will use in the final movie. Click OK.

3. Start Adobe Photoshop, and open the filmstrip file. (If you're using Adobe Photoshop 2.0, choose Acquire/Filmstrip from the File menu to open the filmstrip file.)

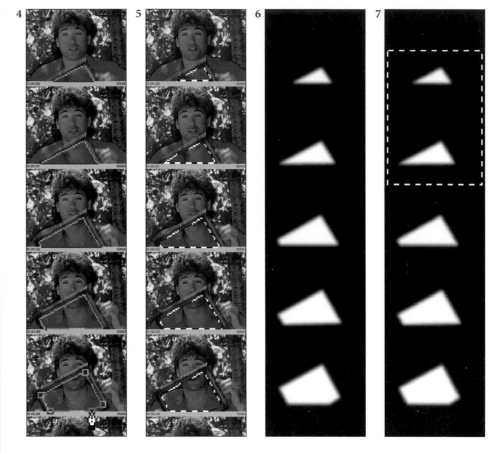

4. Zoom in on the area of the filmstrip that you want to change, and select it. In this example, we wanted to add a special effect to the picture frame that the man is raising to his face. We started by using the pen tool to select that area in each frame of the filmstrip.

5. Once all the paths have been created, choose Save Path and then Make Selection from the Paths palette menu. In this example, we used a Feather Radius of 1 and an anti-aliased edge for a soft-edged selection.

6. If necessary, apply the Motion Blur filter to the selection so that the edges of the selection look natural in the moving picture. (In this example, we needed to apply the filter to the first few frames of the movie, in which the selection moves very fast.) Choose Save Selection/*New* from the Select menu to save the selection in a channel. Do not save over channel #4. If you do not want to apply a filter, skip to step 10.

7. Click channel #5 in the Channels palette. Deselect (⌘D), and then select the frames that you want to blur.

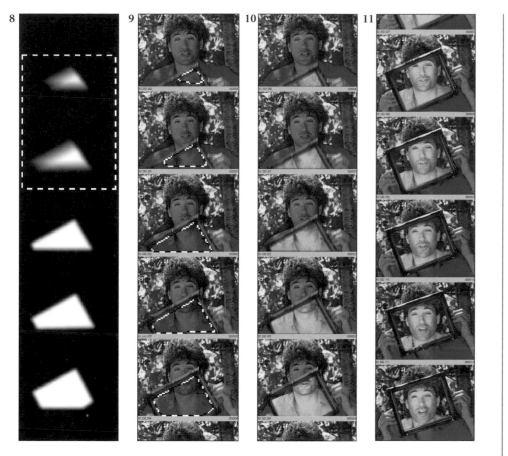

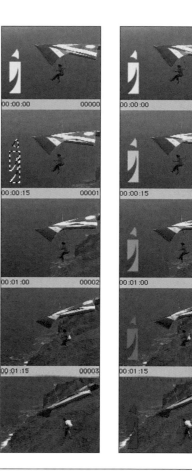

8. From the Filter menu, choose Blur/Motion Blur. Drag the dial in the Motion Blur dialog box until the angle matches the angle at which the selection is moving in the filmstrip. In this example, we used an angle of −60° and a blur amount of 10 pixels. Click OK.

9. Deselect, and return to the RGB channel (⌘0). From the Select menu, choose Load Selection/#5.

10. Choose Hide Edges from the Select menu (⌘H), and apply the special effect you want to the selection. In this example, we used the Hue/Saturation dialog box to change the color of the picture frame.

11. Save the file. If you've saved your selections as paths, they are saved with the file. If you have an extended keyboard and Adobe Photoshop 2.5, you can view the filmstrip frame by frame by holding down the Shift key and pressing the Page Up or Page Down key.

❧ *Copying selections between frames*

If you're using Adobe Photoshop to modify a selected area of a filmstrip, you may want to copy the selection to the same position in several consecutive frames. To do this, position the selection where you want it in the first frame of the filmstrip; then hold down ⌘-Option-Shift and press the Down Arrow key to copy the selection to the next frame.

Rotating three-dimensional graphics in Adobe Premiere

Software needed: Adobe Illustrator 3.0, Adobe Dimensions 1.0, Adobe Premiere 2.0

This technique demonstrates how to generate a sequence of rotated graphics that can be placed into a Adobe Premiere movie for commercial advertisement comps or multimedia presentations. In this example we rotate extruded graphics; start with step 9 if you intend to use flat artwork or a different type of three-dimensional artwork. You can also use this technique to perform other types of transformations instead of (or in addition to) rotation. Before you start, you should know the movie frame size and the number of frames per second. A good speed for animated graphics in Adobe Premiere is 15 frames per second (fps).

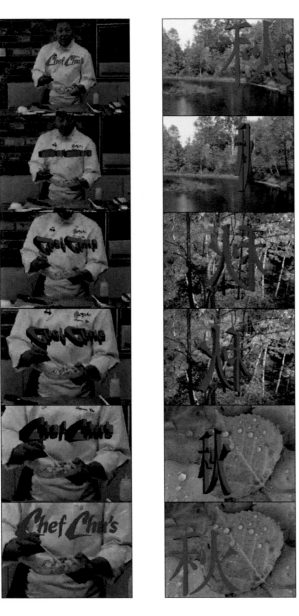

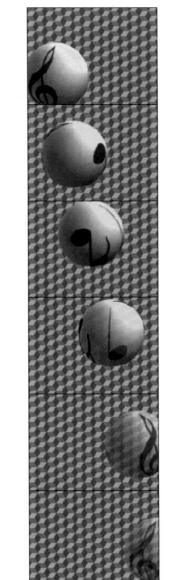

1. Start in Adobe Illustrator by making a box with a width-to-height ratio of 4:3 (called the aspect ratio), about the same size as your movie frame. (We used 120 points by 90 points.) Since you'll use the box only as a visual reference to help you design your graphics and not as part of the artwork, make the box a guide (⌘5).

2. Create your graphics within the guide, with no background. (You'll create a background in a later step.) If you use type, remember to adjust the letterspacing and to create outlines. Paint the graphics (⌘I); keep in mind that anything painted white will become transparent in Adobe Premiere. Save the file as *graphic.ai*.

3. Create a folder for your animation sequences. Open the *graphic.ai* file in Adobe Dimensions, and select the artwork.

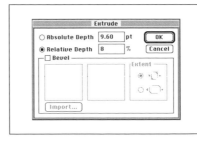

4. Choose Extrude from the Operations menu (⌘-Shift-E). Experiment with different depth amounts to get the results you want. For simple graphics, you may also want a bevel. See the Adobe Dimensions user guide for information on bevels.

5. Make sure that the artwork is still selected; then choose Draft Render to preview (⌘Y).

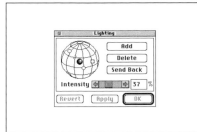

6. Adjust the Lighting (⌘L). Because the artwork will be rotated 360°, you may want to add a highlight to the back. Click Add, and then click Send Back. In this example, we lowered the intensity of the back light. Click Apply when you have finished. To view the back of the graphic, select Back View (⌘2).

7. Now adjust the Surface Properties (⌘I). To make the graphic appear hard and shiny, select Reflectance and then Plastic; then adjust the Matte and Gloss percentages. For a soft, diffused appearance, select Diffuse. Enter the correct number of blends for your artwork using the guidelines on pages 14–17. Then click Apply.

8. The graphic is now ready for you to create the sequence. Return to Artwork mode (⌘W). From the View menu, choose Perspective/Normal and View Angle/Front (⌘1). Save the file before you create the sequence.

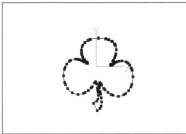

9. With the artwork selected, choose Generate Sequence from the Operations menu; then click OK in the message box. (The Operations menu item in the menu bar remains highlighted.) Select the rotate-dialog tool in the toolbox, click once, and enter 90° in either the *x* or *y* axis box. Then click Apply. When rotating artwork 360°, you must use at least four 90° increments.

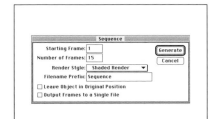

10. Now choose End Sequence from the Operations menu. In this example, we assigned 15 frames to the first rotation so that at a frame rate of 15 frames per second the entire sequence would be four seconds long. Select Shaded Render as the Render Style, and click Generate. Save the files in the folder you created for the sequences in step 3.

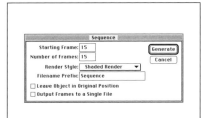

11. Repeat steps 9 and 10; however, change the Starting Frame number to 15. When you are prompted to replace existing files, click Replace. This step compensates for the fact that the new starting frame is always the same as the ending frame of the last sequence. Leaving both frames in the movie creates a pause in the action.

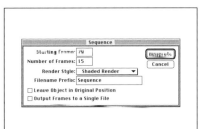

12. Repeat steps 9 and 10 two more times, each time changing the Starting Frame number to the ending frame number of the previous sequence (29 and 43, respectively). With the fourth sequence, your graphic has been rotated 360° and is in its original position. Save the filmstrip (⌘S) with a suffix of *.clip*.

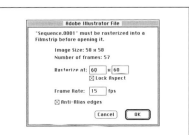

13. Switch to Adobe Premiere, and open the first file in the sequence that you generated. Enter the size at which to rasterize the file, and the frame rate. Adobe Premiere builds the set of four sequences into one filmstrip.

14. In Adobe Premiere, position the pointer over the image in the Clip window until the hand pointer appears. Drag the clip down to the S1 (Superimpose) track in the Construction Window. Save the clip as *rotate.clip*.

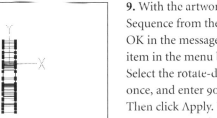

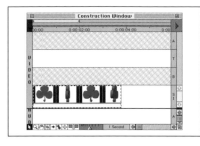

15. Depending on its size, the graphic may become distorted to fit the frame proportions. To correct this, select the filmstrip on the S1 track and choose Maintain Aspect Ratio from the Clip menu (⌘'). Adobe Premiere adjusts the aspect ratio by adding black space around the graphic.

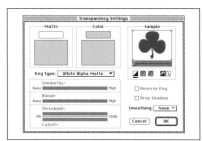

16. To superimpose the graphic onto a different background, you must first remove the background from the filmstrip. While the clip is still selected, choose Transparency from the Clip menu (⌘T). From the Key Type menu, choose White Alpha Matte. This key type removes the white "halo" left over from the background. Click OK.

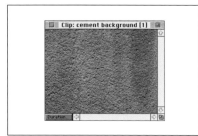

17. Open the image or video clip that you want to use as the background for your rotation sequence. You can use a video clip, a still image, or just a fill. To use an Adobe Photoshop image, simply open the file.

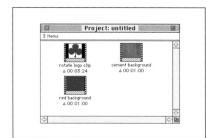

18. Drag the clip into the Project window. If you want a flat color matte as a background, choose Add Color Matte from the Project menu. Select a background color using the Color Picker (⌘-), and click OK. Name the background, and click OK again. The background appears as a clip icon in the Project window.

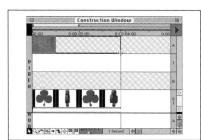

19. Drag the background clip from the Project window to track A. If you are using a color matte or a still image, drag the right edge of the clip to extend the full length of the sequence. The right edge of the clip on track A should be aligned with the right edge of the clip on track S1.

20. Drag the yellow work area bar at the top of the Construction window so that it extends the length of the sequence. Save the project.

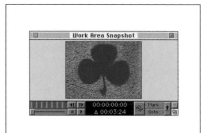

21. For a quick preview of the rotation sequence, press Enter. For a higher quality preview, choose Snapshot from the Make menu (⌘\). This command creates a snapshot movie of the clips under the work area bar.

❧ *Copying a filter effect to all clips on a track*

You can use the Paste Special command in Adobe Premiere to copy a filter effect from one clip to all clips on that track.

After you've applied the filter to a clip, select the clip and copy it to the Clipboard. Select the next clip on the track, and choose Paste Special from the Edit menu (⌘H). In the Paste Special dialog box, click Settings and then Paste. Now select the track tool, and select the entire track.

Choose Paste Special Again from the Edit menu (⌘R) to apply the filter to all clips on the track.

6

Color Reproduction in Adobe Photoshop

Color Reproduction in Adobe Photoshop

Color reproduction in Adobe Photoshop

Software needed: Adobe Photoshop 2.0

Getting the color in your Adobe Photoshop images to appear exactly as you want can be a tricky process. A number of factors are essential to precise color reproduction, including the calibration of your scanner, imagesetter, and workstation; the quality of the original image or scan; the type of separation you use; and the skill of the color operator. This section provides a brief overview of what you need to successfully reproduce color images, and then outlines steps for color correcting an image. Be sure to read the section on calibration before you try following the steps. If your system is miscalibrated, you can't color correct in RGB mode.

Calibration

A color reproduction system is calibrated when all components of the system—for example, the scanner, imagesetter, and workstation—agree both numerically and visually. Using Adobe Photoshop's calibration tools ensures that the image on your screen matches your printed output. Once you have this match, you can compensate for color and contrast problems in the image by color correcting the image. If the match doesn't exist, you can't use the image on-screen to perform color corrections.

Adobe Photoshop's calibration tools do two things: 1) they affect how images appear on-screen and 2) they determine how Photoshop converts colors from RGB to CMYK. *If you have not calibrated your system, you must perform all color corrections in CMYK mode.* Because CMYK images are significantly larger than RGB images, color correcting in CMYK mode can be much more time-consuming. In addition, if your system isn't calibrated, you can't color correct *visually*—your output won't match the image on-screen. In this case, you must color correct *numerically* using target CMYK values.

Adobe Photoshop's calibration settings are in the Preferences dialog boxes under the File menu. In most cases, the default calibration settings produce excellent results. (The examples in this section were created using Photoshop's default settings.) It's important, however, to calibrate your monitor and to change your settings to compensate for any unusual output conditions, such as special printing inks or uncoated paper stock. To calibrate your system, follow the step-by-step instructions in chapter 15 of the Adobe Photoshop user guide.

```
General...              ⌘K
Function Keys...
Plug-ins...
Scratch Disks...
Units...

Monitor Setup...
Printing Inks Setup...
Separation Setup...
Separation Tables...
```

Preferences commands

Scanning

An often-quoted rule for working with scanned images is "garbage in, garbage out." To some extent, your scanner controls and Adobe Photoshop can compensate for flaws in the original image. However, if image details aren't captured during scanning, it's difficult, if not impossible, to achieve good final output.

To ensure that minimal color information has been lost in the scanning process, it's a good idea to check the pixel values of your highlight and shadow areas after scanning. To do this, open the Info palette and use the eyedropper to measure the values of the lightest highlight areas that contain detail in the image and the darkest shadow areas that contain detail. As a rule of thumb, RGB highlight values of about 240 and shadow values of about 10 indicate that the scan contains enough detail to produce good results.

In addition, if you're not sure of your final output size or resolution, it's a good idea to scan the image at a higher resolution than you need for your output, and then resample the image later. A resolution of about twice the line screen is recommended for high quality output. See chapter 2 of the Adobe Photoshop user guide for other guidelines on determining the correct scanning resolution.

One more useful tip for scanning is to scan a gray wedge with your image. If your image does not contain any gray, the gray wedge will enable you to easily correct a color cast introduced by scanning (see page 93).

Color correction

Adobe Photoshop includes a number of tools for adjusting or correcting color. Some of these tools—such as Color Balance, Variations, and Brightness/Contrast—are designed for quick and easy color correction with adequate results. For high quality color reproduction, however, the tools used in this section are recommended.

Note that depending on your image, you may not need to perform certain procedures described in the following sections. For example, you may not need to adjust the midtones after correcting the highlights and shadows, or you may not need to adjust the color after correcting the overall contrast.

STEPS TO COLOR REPRODUCTION

1. Make sure that your system is calibrated and check the quality of your scan (page 88).

2. Identify the key type of your image (page 89).

3. Adjust the highlights and shadows (page 89).

4. Adjust the midtones and fine-tune the contrast (page 91).

5. Correct the overall color balance in the image (page 93).

6. Sharpen the image using the Unsharp Mask filter (page 94).

7. After converting to CMYK, fine-tune the color corrections (page 95).

Identifying the image key type

Before you begin color correcting an image, identify the type of image you are working with. The lightness or darkness of an image is sometimes referred to as its *key type*. Identifying the image key type tells you where the detail is in the image and helps you make decisions on contrast adjustments.

In the following steps we will color correct three images: one is a light, or high key image; one is a dark, or low key, image; and one is an average image. Looking at the histogram in the Levels dialog box for each of these images, you can see how the pixels in the image are distributed. The heavy distribution of pixels in the histogram indicates where the detail is in the image; the lack of pixels in the histogram indicates where detail is lacking. Notice that for all three images the pixels in the histograms are more evenly distributed after color correction, indicating an increase in the overall tonal range .

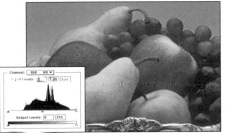

Average key image: pixels concentrated in midtones.

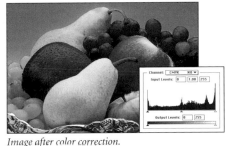

Image after color correction.

High key image: pixels concentrated in highlights.

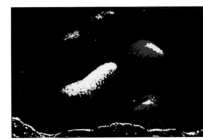

Image after color correction.

Low key image: pixels concentrated in shadows.

Image after color correction.

Adjusting the highlights and shadows

After you've checked your Preferences calibration settings, the first procedure in color correction is to identify and assign a value to the lightest and darkest areas in the image. This adjustment defines the tonal range of the image and is the primary contrast adjustment.

1. Double-click the eyedropper tool and change the Point Sample size to a 3 by 3 average pixel area. This step ensures that your adjustments are based on a true sample of the area you click rather than an individual pixel value.

2. Now identify the highlights in the image. With some images, the location of the highlights is obvious; if you have any doubts, use one of these tips to help you locate the lightest part of the image:

■ In the Levels dialog box, hold down the Option key and drag the right Input triangle slowly toward the left. (Make sure that the Preview option is not selected.) The areas that first appear white in the image are the lightest areas in the image.

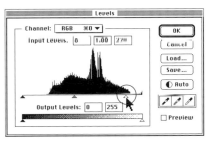

Using Levels with Option key to identify highlights. First visible areas indicate highlights.

■ In the Curves dialog box, move the eyedropper around the image and watch the circle on the curve. When the circle is closest to the highlight end of the curve (and the density reading is at its lowest), you've located the light areas in the image.

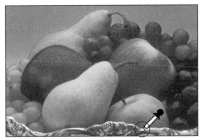

Using Curves to identify highlights. Pixel's position displayed on curve and numerically below the curve.

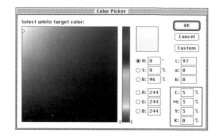

3. Double-click the white eyedropper button in the Levels or Curves dialog box, and enter your target "white" value in the Color Picker. Remember that this white should be printable white; not the white that results from no ink on the page, called "specular" white. A typical printable white is created by CMY percentages of 5, 3, and 3, respectively. Click OK.

4. Now click the highlight area you identified in step 2 to set those pixel values to 5, 3, 3. Any pixel values whiter than the highlight pixels become specular white. In this example, we used a highlight value of 5, 3, 3 for the average and high key type images. For the low key type image, we used a value of 7, 3, 3 to darken the highlight and hold the detail in the paper. If your image contains very burned-out white, try using even higher values.

5. Locate the shadows using one of the techniques given in step 2. With Levels, hold down the Option key and drag the left triangle to the right. (Remember to make sure that the Preview option is not selected.) The areas that first appear black are the shadow areas.

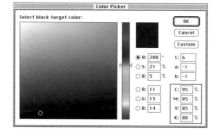

6. Double-click the black eyedropper in Levels or Curves and enter a target shadow value. Traditional target shadow percentages are CMYK 95, 85, 85, and 80. Click OK.

7. Click the shadow area you identified in step 5. In our examples, we used a shadow value of 95, 85, 85, and 80 in all three images.

Note: *Adobe Photoshop's color separation tools automatically adjust the ink values so that total ink coverage does not exceed 300% after separation.*

Original image.

Highlights set by clicking non-neutral glare in jewelry.

Highlights set by clicking white in pupil.

Highlights set by clicking highlight in hair; pixels in pupil become specular white.

Choose a true highlight and shadow area to maintain detail in the image. While adjusting the highlights and shadows in an image is often referred to as "setting the white and black point," this phrase can be misleading. Choosing a white or black color in the image, rather than a true highlight or shadow area, can result in loss of detail in the highlights or shadows. In addition, choosing a non-neutral, or tinted, shadow or highlight area can throw off the color in the image. Try clicking a few white and black points in the image until you get the contrast adjustment you want.

Adjusting the midtones and fine-tuning the contrast

At this point you may want to further fine-tune the contrast by adjusting the midtones. This step may not be necessary: with average key type images, for example, setting the white and black points is often the only contrast adjustment needed. In high and low key images, however, you may want to adjust the midtones to balance the overall contrast in the image.

1. Adjust the midtones using Levels or Curves. Curves gives you more precise control over the results since you can adjust any point along the curve. On the other hand, unless your adjustments are extremely precise, you may find it easier to use Levels. Continue to step 2 before clicking OK.

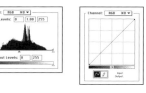
Average key type image: no additional midtone adjustment necessary.

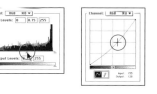
High key image: Levels midtone slider adjusted to .75 to darken the midtones and increase the detail in the highlights. Same adjustment shown in Curves.

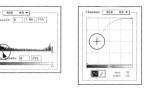
Low key image: Levels midtone slider adjusted to 1.9 to lighten the midtones and increase the detail in the shadows. Same adjustment shown in Curves.

Like Curves, Levels works by defining two sets of values: Current density values (input values) and desired density values (output values). You can adjust either set of values. To understand how Levels works, it's helpful to create an 11-step gray wedge and watch the effect as you adjust the Levels controls.

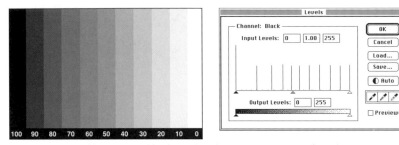

Gray wedge created by creating a blend and then choosing Map/Posterize from the Image menu. Pixels distributed in 11 distinct positions in the Levels histogram.

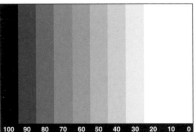 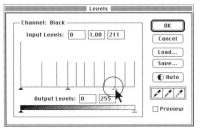

Levels highlight slider moved to the second position from the right. Notice that all color is removed from those areas in the gray wedge.

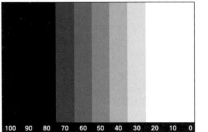 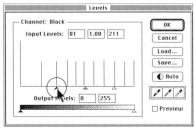

Levels highlight slider moved to the second position from the left. Notice that all color is removed from those areas in the gray wedge.

2. If necessary, fine-tune the white and black points until the effect is as you want it. You can change the eyedropper values and reset the highlights and shadows, or use Levels or Curves to adjust the contrast. In this example, we used Levels to create a darker black in the robes and enhance the detail in the shadow.

 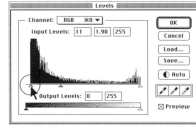

Curves let you adjust any range of values while keeping other values fixed. A common contrast adjustment is represented by an S-curve, where the highlights and shadows are adjusted in opposite directions. For a flat photograph, an S-curve is created by making the highlights lighter and the shadows darker, as in the example shown here. For a photograph with too much contrast, the inverse of this curve would give good results.

Flat RGB image.

Curves adjusted to increase highlights and shadows.

Adjusting the color balance

After adjusting the contrast, you're ready to correct the color in the image.

1. First adjust for any overall color cast in the image usng Curves. In the Curves dialog box, select the channel in which the color seems too dominant. (In our example, the average key image had a slight blue cast and the low key image had a slight red cast.) Move the pointer to the area in the image containing the cast—if possible, select a gray area in the image—and note where the area falls on the curve. Click the points on the curve you want to remain stationary (see the Sidebar at bottom right), and then drag the point that needs adjustment.

The goal of this step is to create *neutral* grays in the image, that is, gray values that contain equal parts of red, green, and blue. You will adjust the color in the image in the next step.

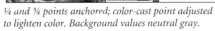

Blue channel selected; blue cast in background located on curve.

¼ and ¾ points anchored; color-cast point adjusted to lighten color. Background values neutral gray.

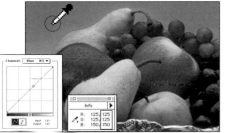

No color cast adjustment necessary.

Red channel selected; red cast in faces located on curve.

Midpoint and ¼ point anchored; color-cast point adjusted to lighten color.

2. Now use Hue/Saturation to adjust the individual colors in the image. Click the color in the image that needs adjustment to copy that color into the Hue/Saturation sample box. Then select the color component option that you want to adjust, and use the sliders to adjust the color.

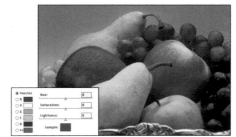

Image lacking overall saturation and color.

Saturation increased for Master. Hue adjusted for R, Y, G, and B to bring up fruit color.

Red weak in strawberries and honey; yellow weak in wood and bread.

Saturation increased for R and Y. Hue adjusted to incease magenta in R and reduce red in Y.

Heavy red in faces. Color weak in trees and in woman's hair.

Hue adjusted to reduce magenta in R, red in Y, and yellow in G. Saturation increased for R.

Anchoring points on the Curve helps you isolate adjustments to specific tonal areas.
For example, you may want to anchor the midpoint so that you can adjust the highlights without affecting the shadows. To anchor a point on the Curve, simply click the place on the curve that you want to remain fixed. Note that areas between fixed points are still slightly affected by the adjustment.

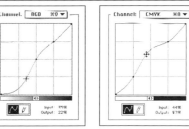

Midpoint and ¾ point fixed to adjust ¼ tones.

¼ and ¾ points fixed to adjust midtones.

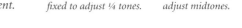
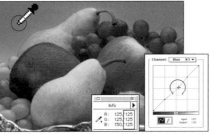

Conceptually, Hue/Saturation controls are based on the color wheel. Moving around the color wheel represents a hue adjustment and moving across the diameter of the wheel represents a saturation adjustment. When you select a color option in the Hue/Saturation dialog box, the two adjacent colors on the color wheel are displayed on either side of the Hue slider. By giving you isolated control over each color component, Hue/Saturation lets you simulate true selective color correction.

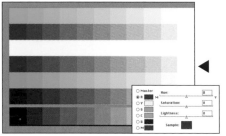

Photoshop file containing bands of 100% C, M, Y, R, G, and B.

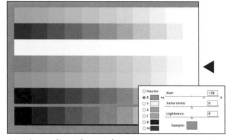

Hue in R adjusted away from M, removing magenta from red band. Magenta band remains unaltered.

In general, an Unsharp Mask amount of 150 works well for most high-resolution images. *For very high-resolution images above 300 pixels per inch), you may want to increase the Amount up to 200. Leave the Radius value at 1. If you're working with an image that contains very subtle changes between pixels on a single surface (such as a face), experiment with a Threshold value between 2 and 20. The Threshold option tells Photoshop not to sharpen an area unless the change in pixel values exceeds the threshold value. Be sure to print a proof to check the effect of different sharpening values. The effect of sharpening appears much more dramatic on-screen than in a printed image.*

Unsharp Mask: Threshold 20

Unsharp Mask: Threshold 0

Sharpening the image

Once you have completed your RGB color corrections, use the Unsharp Mask filter to sharpen the image. Sharpening compensates for some of the blurring introduced by scanning and printing. While you can apply the Unsharp Mask filter in RGB or CMYK mode, applying the filter in RGB mode requires less memory.

Apply the Unsharp Mask filter to the image, using the dialog box values shown here as a starting point (see Sidebar at left). If you're experimenting with different Unsharp Mask values, be sure to choose the Undo command before reapplying the filter. In our three examples, we used an Amount of 150, a Radius of 1, and varied the Threshold amount.

Before Unsharp Mask.

Unsharp Mask applied; Threshold 4.

Before Unsharp Mask.

Unsharp Mask applied; Threshold 2.

Before Unsharp Mask.

Unsharp Mask applied; Threshold 10.

Fine-tuning the corrections

After converting to CMYK mode, you may want to perform additional adjustments using Curves. In our low key image, we used Curves to remove some unwanted magenta introduced back into the image in the separation process.

1. Click the bar below the bottom of the curve to put the Curves dialog box in CMYK mode (see Sidebar below). In the Curves dialog box, select the color channel you want to adjust. Move the pointer to the color area in the image that you want to change, and note where that area falls on the curve. In this example, the face colors fell in the midtones.

2. Click to anchor points at parts of the curve you don't want to adjust—in our example, we fixed points for the ¼ and ¾ tones. Then drag to make the adjustment. Keep in mind that small curve adjustments may have a dramatic impact on overall color in the image.

If you're working in RGB mode, work with the curve in its default state. This way the curve moves from shadows on the left to highlights on the white. This way the input and output values match RGB values: a value of 0 represents complete shadow and a value of 255 represents extreme highlight. Dragging the ¾ point up increases the highlights.

Curves dialog box in RGB mode.

When your image is in CMYK mode, click the bar beneath the curve to transpose the graph. Now the curve moves from highlights on the left to shadows on the right. Values are displayed in percentages and so match CMYK values: a value of 0% represents extreme highlight and a value of 100% represents complete shadow. Dragging the ¾ point up increases the shadows.

Curves dialog box in CMYK mode.

❧ *Performing isolated color adjustments*

In some cases, you may want to create a mask to adjust the color within a given area. You can use the procedure described here at the fine-tuning stage to adjust the color of individual objects in the image. You can also use this procedure to dramatically change the color of an object—in this case, it's best to make the adjustment before fine-tuning so that you can see the effect of the new color on the overall image.

1. Select the object whose color you want to change. In this sample we selected the girl's red hat and saved it in a channel.

2. Choose your target color. If you know the CMYK value you want, enter the value into the Color Picker. (In this example, we selected the color of the girl's shirt from the image.) Write down the HSB equivalents of your target CMYK value. The Hue value represents the number of degrees the hue is on the Color Wheel from red, the 0° point. Click OK.

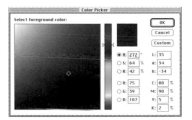

3. Open the Hue/Saturation dialog box and click Colorize. Colorize resets the hues to the 0 point on the color wheel (red) and the saturation to 100%. The lightness values of the pixels are preserved. Enter the Hue and Saturation value you wrote down in step 2. If the hue value you wrote down is greater than 180, subtract 360 from that value and enter the negative result. (In our example, we entered 272–360, or 88.) Do not enter a Brightness value.

4. Click OK. The slection is painted with the new color and the brightness value of the pixels are preserved.

TARGET CMYK PRINTING VALUES					
CMYK COLOR MIX	COLOR SWATCH	C	M	Y	K
NEUTRAL HIGHLIGHT		5	3	3	0
NEUTRAL SHADOW		95	85	85	80
DEEP VIOLET		100	68	10	25
DEEP PURPLE		85	95	10	0
SKY BLUE		60	23	0	0
AQUA		60	0	25	0
KELLY GREEN		100	0	100	0
LEMON YELLOW		5	18	75	0
GOLD		5	15	65	0
ORANGE RED		10	100	100	0
ORANGE		5	50	100	0
DEEP RED		25	100	80	0
PINK		5	40	5	0
BEIGE		5	5	15	0

TARGET CMYK PRINTING VALUES					
CMYK COLOR MIX	COLOR SWATCH	C	M	Y	K
CAUCASIAN FLESH		18	45	50	0
ASIAN FLESH		15	40	55	0
BLACK FLESH		35	45	50	28
CHOCOLATE BROWN		45	65	100	38
DARK BLACK		95	87	87	80
GRAY		55	42	42	15
SILVER		20	15	14	0

If you're color correcting numerically rather than visually, you'll need to start with target CMYK values. You can also use these values to check whether your corrected color values displayed in the Info palette are within range of target printing values. Remember that the values in this chart are only guidelines and that color percentages may vary significantly. Also keep in mind that the relationship, or ratio, between the color components is more important than the individual values in determining the hue. For example, to produce a lighter Caucasian fleshtone than the color shown in this chart, be sure to reduce the C, M, Y, and K values by an equal percentage.

If you're checking gray values in CMYK mode, keep in mind that equal parts of C, M, and Y produce neutral gray in theory only. In reality, cyan is assigned a slightly higher value than magenta and yellow for most press conditions. The percent incease in cyan varies with where the gray is in the tonal range. Use these guidelines to determine how much higher than magenta and yellow the cyan value should be to produce neutral gray:

- *For highlights: 3%–5% higher*
- *For ¼ tones: 7%–10% higher*
- *For midtones: 10%–15% higher*
- *For ¾ tones: 8%–12% higher*
- *For shadows: 7%–10% higher*

7 Printing and Production

Working with clipping paths

*Combining Adobe Illustrator and Adobe
  Photoshop artwork*

*Comparing Adobe Illustrator and Adobe
  Photoshop output*

Working with clipping paths

Software needed: Adobe Photoshop 2.0

Original Photoshop image.

Background "deleted" in Photoshop.

EPS image placed in Illustrator with no clipping path.

Preview of image: EPS image background opaque.

EPS image placed in Illustrator with clipping path.

Preview of image: EPS image background transparent.

Often when your project is designed for process color printing, you'll want to create color separations in Adobe Photoshop and then import the file into an illustration program, such as Adobe Illustrator, or a page-layout application, such as QuarkXPress®. In general, the best way to transfer CMYK files between Adobe Photoshop and these programs is to first save the file in Encapsulated PostScript (EPS) format. If you want to import just a selection from the Photoshop file, you'll need to first define the selection as a clipping path.

A clipping path is a path that makes the background of an Adobe Photoshop selection transparent when the image is printed or previewed in another application. You create clipping paths by creating the path around the image that you want to place, defining the path as a clipping path, and then saving the file in EPS format. When the EPS file with the clipping path is placed in another application, such as Adobe Illustrator, the Photoshop image surrounding the clipping path does not display or print.

Creating a clipping path

1. In Adobe Photoshop, choose Show Paths from the Window menu to display the Paths palette.

2. Draw a path with the pen tool, or make a selection with another selection tool and then choose Make Path from the Paths palette menu. Choose Save Path from the Paths palette menu, and name the path.

3. Choose Clipping Path from the Paths palette menu. In the Clipping Path dialog box, select the path that you just saved.

4. If your path is complex, enter a Flatness setting. (See "Avoiding Printing Problems" on page 99 for information on complex paths and Flatness settings.)

5. Choose one of the following options, depending on whether the path is compound or simple. These options help the PostScript printer simplify the path.

- If the path is a compound path (such as a cut-out caused by positive and negative spaces, or a path with intersecting lines), select the Even-Odd Fill Rule option.

- If the path is simple (a single path without intersecting lines), select the Non-Zero Winding Fill Rule option.

6. Click OK. If you plan to print the file using process colors, convert the file to CMYK mode. Save the file in EPS format. In most situations, you should leave the EPS Format dialog box settings at their default values. See chapter 2 of the Adobe Photoshop user guide for information on changing the dialog box settings.

7. Start your illustration or page-layout program, open the file in which you will place the Photoshop image, and place the EPS file. Preview the image.

Avoiding printing problems with clipping paths

A common problem with clipping paths is that the paths are too complex to print. If your clipping path is too complex, the printer may generate a "limitcheck" error or a general PostScript® error—or the printer may just not recognize the path.

A complex path is a path that is described by multiple line segments and anchor points. Because of its coarser grid, a low-resolution printer uses fewer line segments to describe a curve than a high-resolution printer. This means that a complex path that has printed on a low-resolution printer—because the printer has automatically simplified the path—may not print on a high-resolution device.

The key to simplifying a path is to reduce the number of anchor points on the path. Use these guidelines to simplify your clipping paths:

- If the path was created using the Make Path command, delete the path, increase the tolerance in the Make Path dialog box, and then choose Make Path again. The higher the tolerance, the fewer anchor points used to convert the selection, and the smoother the path. Remember that changing the tolerance affects the path only when you choose the Make Path command, not after the selection has been converted to a path.

Tolerance: 1 pixel

Tolerance: 4 pixels

- Redraw your path with the pen tool, or use the delete-anchor-point tool to remove any unnecessary anchor points from the path.

- Simplify the path by increasing the Flatness setting in the Clipping Path dialog box. A high Flatness setting tells the PostScript interpreter to "flatten" the curve when printed. In general, a Flatness setting of from 8 to 10 is recommended for high-resolution printing (1200 dpi to 2400 dpi); a setting of from 1 to 3 is recommended for low-resolution printing (300 dpi to 600 dpi).

Flatness: 0

Flatness: 30

Saving selections as paths

If you're using a version of Adobe Photoshop earlier than 2.5.1 and your file contains multiple selections, you can help keep your file size to a minimum by saving the selections as paths instead of in channels. The saved paths do not affect the placement or printing of the file unless the path is saved in EPS format as a clipping path. Keep in mind, however, that using the Make Path command eliminates any feathering applied to the selection and may alter the shape of the path. You can redefine the feather edge when you choose the Make Selection command in the Paths palette; however, the effect will change slightly.

If you're using Adobe Photoshop 2.5.1, the program automatically compresses large areas of flat color, and so minimizes any increase in file size caused by saving selections in channels.

Combining Adobe Illustrator and Adobe Photoshop artwork

When sharing artwork between Adobe Photoshop and Adobe Illustrator, it's important to understand that Photoshop is raster-based and Illustrator is vector-based. This means that in Adobe Photoshop objects are described as pixels on a raster, or grid; while in Adobe Illustrator, objects are mathematically described as vectors. Vector-based graphics generate crisp, clear lines when scaled to any size. Raster-based programs are typically better for working with organic shapes, such as those in photographs.

Using Adobe Illustrator artwork in Adobe Photoshop

When you open an Illustrator file in Photoshop, Photoshop rasterizes the vector-based Illustrator file, transforming the crisp, clean curves into digital curves. All layering, grouping, patterns, and gradient fills are discarded. You can determine whether the image is rasterized using anti-aliased edges by selecting the Anti-alias PostScript option in the General Preferences dialog box. By default, this option is on. While anti-aliasing can make the edges of objects appear fuzzy, it is generally preferable to the "stair-stepping" appearance that occurs without it. On the other hand, if your artwork consists of vertical and horizontal lines and no curves, you can achieve better results without anti-aliasing.

Adobe Illustrator

Adobe Photoshop, anti-aliased

Photoshop, anti-aliased off

You can bring Illustrator graphics and type into Photoshop using one of four methods:

Place command. The Place command lets you easily resize graphics and type without sacrificing quality. When you use the Place command to bring in the image, the image appears on-screen in a box with highlighted corners. Drag the corners to scale the image; Photoshop does not rasterize the image until you click the gavel icon. The advantage to using Place command is that it imports the image with no background pixels and adapts the image to the current resolution of the Photoshop file. Most importantly, you can scale the image before it is rasterized. If you scale the image after it is rasterized, the edges may begin to deteriorate and degrade the image quality.

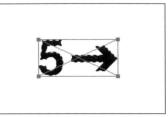

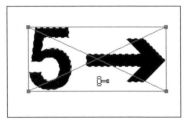

Copy and paste from the Clipboard. If you own Adobe Photoshop 2.5 and Adobe Illustrator 5.0, you can copy the type or graphics from your Illustrator file to the Clipboard, and then switch to Photoshop and paste the graphics. This method has the advantages of convenience and speed: you don't need to save separate files. When you paste the objects, Photoshop rasterizes them at their size in the Illustrator file.

For example, if you copy an Illustrator graphic that is 2 inches wide and 3 inches tall and paste it into Photoshop, Photoshop will rasterize it at 2 inches by 3 inches at the current resolution of the file. The disadvantage of using this method is that if you want to scale the type once it's in Photoshop, you will lose quality. To maintain image quality, return to Illustrator, scale the type, and then copy and paste it again into Photoshop.

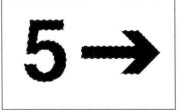

Open an Illustrator file in Photoshop. If you're brining an entire design or layout into Photoshop, it's easiest to just open the Illustrator file using Photoshop's Open command. When you open an Illustrator file in Photoshop, the EPS Rasterizer dialog box appears. If you plan to combine this image with other Photoshop images, make sure that the resolution of the new file matches that of the other files. You can then use the file to copy and paste elements into Photoshop files. Remember to rename the rasterized Illustrator file so that you don't accidentally write over the original file.

Bring an Illustrator graphic into a channel. If you want to use type or a graphic as a building block for creating a more complex design in Photoshop, place or copy the artwork into a new channel of the Photoshop image. You can then experiment with the graphic as a mask in Photoshop. When you create the artwork in Illustrator, be sure to paint it black and white if you want the mask to be opaque. If any of the graphics are painted, they will become a percentage of gray when pasted into a channel and create a semitransparent mask.

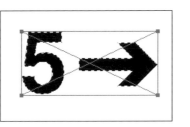

To create the channel, choose New Channel from the Channels palette. Use the Place command or the Clipboard to bring the type or graphic into the new channel. Once the graphic is in the new channel, deselect it (⌘D), and choose Map/Invert from the Image menu (⌘I) to make a negative of the image. (The selection is defined by the white area.)

To view the selection with the other graphics in your file, select the composite image channel in the Channels palette, and choose Load Selection from the Select menu. To reposition the selection, hold down the Command and Option keys and drag the selection. Holding down the Command and Option keys enables you to drag just the selection border, not the pixels within the selection. When you are satisfied with the new position, choose Save Selection from the Select menu to save the repositioned selection back to the channel.

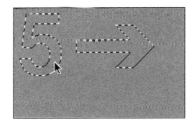

Using Adobe Photoshop paths in Adobe Illustrator

Although Adobe Photoshop is a raster-based program, you can create and save vector-based curves using the pen tool or the Make Path command. You use this feature to save a selection or mask as a path in Adobe Photoshop and then bring it into Adobe Illustrator to create a graphic or effect that can't be achieved in Photoshop. The two images can then be combined again in either Photoshop or Illustrator. In this example, we saved a selection of a flower as a path in Photoshop and exported it to Illustrator. We then used Illustrator's path-type tool to create type on the path so that the type would be perfectly aligned with the Photoshop image. To create the final image, we placed an EPS version of the Photoshop flower behind the type in the Illustrator file.

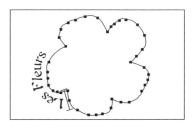

Photoshop paths can be brought into Adobe Illustrator using one of two methods:

Paths to Illustrator. The Paths to Illustrator feature lets you export multiple paths in one step. To use the feature, save the paths in the Photoshop file, and then choose Export/Paths to Illustrator from the File menu. Choose a filename and location, and click Save to save all paths in the Photoshop file to a new Illustrator file.

Copy the path to the Clipboard, and paste it into an Illustrator file. If you're using Adobe Photoshop 2.5, you can copy paths from Photoshop and paste them into Illustrator. Simply select the path in Photoshop, and copy it to the Clipboard. Then switch to Adobe Illustrator and paste the path into your file. Make sure that the entire path selected; only what is selected will be copied. In this example, we brought the flower shape into Illustrator and then filled it with a radial gradient fill.

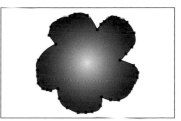

Comparing Adobe Illustrator and Adobe Photoshop output

Once you are proficient in using both Adobe Photoshop and Adobe Illustrator, you can use them together in some very exciting and creative ways. Even though Illustrator is "vector-based" and Photoshop is "raster-based" (see pages 100–101), you can combine the two types of files into one. The first decision you need to make when combining artwork files is whether to use Photoshop or Illustrator for your final output. If the file contains both photographs and type, you'll need to choose between the clean, crisp edges of Illustrator's PostScript language type and the softer, anti-aliased edges that you get with Photoshop. There are many other considerations as well.

Deciding which program to use

Before you start building your file, analyze the elements of the image, and decide which program is best for creating the elements and which for printing them. In general, if your artwork contains type or line art that you want to print with clean, sharp edges, you'll want to print the file from Adobe Illustrator rather than Adobe Photoshop. On the other hand, if you want the entire image to have soft lines or photographic special effects, you'll probably want to print the file from Photoshop.

In most cases, Adobe Illustrator is a better program for laying out your design. Unlike Photoshop artwork, once you deselect artwork in Illustrator, it can easily be reselected and moved, altered, or deleted—common occurrences in the design process. Once you bring the line art, guides, and type into Photoshop, you can add photographs or textures, or use some of the painting tools to add a more painterly look to the piece. Use the following guidelines for help choosing the best program for your output:

Use Photoshop for	Use Illustrator for
Working with and editing photographs	Type (creating, editing, and printing)
Textures	Patterns
Organic shapes	Clean, accurately placed lines and shapes
Painterly or soft lines and strokes	Editing and making changes
Special effects	Multicolored gradient fills
Smudged or blurred lines	Blends between shapes
Masks and silhouettes	Spot colors

Keep in mind that while you can bring a Photoshop file into Illustrator unaltered as an EPS file, any Illustrator graphics you bring into Photoshop will be *rasterized*, or digitized, into pixel-based artwork with anti-aliased edges. In addition, any Illustrator patterns, gradient fills, or spot colors will be replaced in Photoshop with a solid fill.

Comparing the Jazz posters

The illustrations on the facing page show a poster assembled and printed in Adobe Illustrator and then in Adobe Photoshop. To create the Illustrator file, the grayscale Photoshop image was saved in EPS format and placed in Illustrator. We then added type and graphics in Illustrator, and separated the image using Adobe Separator™.

To create the Photoshop file, we first divided the type and graphics into several Illustrator files. We then pasted the grayscale file into an RGB file and placed the Illustrator files individually using the Place command. Because Photoshop doesn't recognize gradient fills from Adobe Illustrator 5.0, the gradient fills were recreated in Photoshop. The file was separated in Photoshop. See pages 100–101 for tips on transferring files between Illustrator and Photoshop.

Note these four key differences between the two files:

Adobe Illustrator version	Adobe Photoshop version
1. CMYK plus one custom spot color	1. Custom color converted to CMYK
2. Illustrator 5.0 gradient fills, including multicolor gradient fills	2. Gradient fills recreated in Photoshop
3. Type and line art edges sharp	3. Type and line art edges slightly fuzzy
4. File size: 13,191K (includes 12,989K EPS file)	4. File size: 9,790K

Because of the clarity of the lines and the smoothness of the gradient fills, you would probably want to use Illustrator to print this poster. One advantage of using Photoshop, however, is the reduction in file size. In Photoshop, the grayscale photograph had a file size of 9,790K. After the file was saved in EPS format, the file size increased to 12,989K. This increase results in an almost 3 MB difference between the two poster files. You can work around this problem by resizing or resampling the Photoshop file and then resaving it in EPS format.

◟ *Editing placed EPS files*

If you're using Adobe Illustrator 5.0, and you want to edit or change a placed EPS file, hold down the Option key, and double-click the placed image. The application that created the file will start and open the file. Make your changes, and then save the document. Illustrator automatically updates the file to the newly edited EPS file.

Adobe Illustrator file

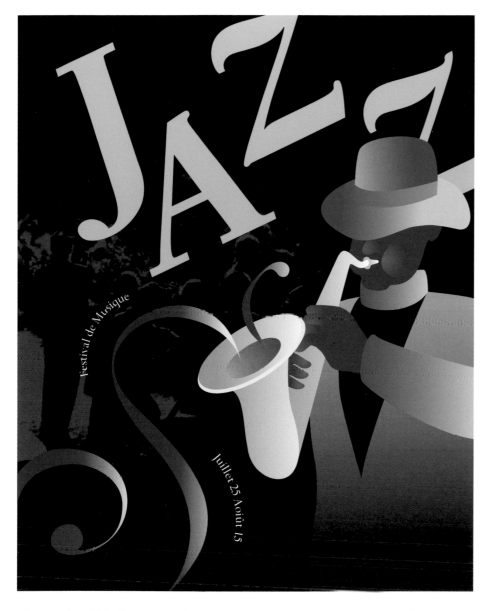

File output from Adobe Illustrator 5.0. The background photo is a 300-dpi, grayscale Photoshop file placed in Illustrator as an EPS file. The "JAZZ" type is a custom ink color, PMS 5517. Gradient fills—including a number of multicolor gradient fills—were created using the gradient fill tool. Typeface: Spectrum™

Adobe Photoshop file

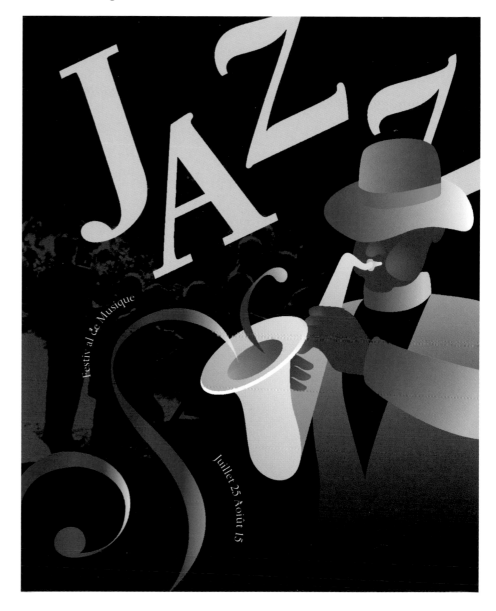

File output from Adobe Photoshop 2.5. The Illustrator artwork from the file shown on the left was brought into a 300-dpi RGB Photoshop file using the Place Art command. The custom color was automatically converted to CMYK equivalents, and the file was separated in Photoshop. Gradients were recreated in Photoshop.

Appendixes

Upgrade notes for Design Essentials

Additional Adobe Illustrator and Adobe
Photoshop tips

Upgrade notes for
Design Essentials

Since the publication of the first book in the Professional Studio Techniques series, Design Essentials, *Adobe Systems has released new versions of Adobe Photoshop (version 2.5 for Macintosh and Windows) and Adobe Illustrator (version 4.0 for Windows; version 5.0 for the Macintosh). In addition, Adobe has introduced Adobe Dimensions, a three-dimensional drawing program on the Macintosh. In most cases, you will find that using the new Adobe software does not significantly change the techniques in* Design Essentials. *Certain effects, however, can be produced more efficiently using Adobe Photoshop 2.5, Adobe Illustrator 5.0, or Adobe Dimensions.*

The following upgrade notes list the techniques in Design Essentials *that may be affected by using the new software and describe an alternative procedure for the technique. Minor changes in the techniques, such as the name of a command, its location in the menu structure, or the new design of a dialog box, are not included in these upgrade notes.*

Shapes with multiple outlines (page 10)

If you're using Adobe Illustrator version 5.0, you can produce this effect more easily using the Offset Path filter in the new Filter menu. (See "Creating Frames and Concentric Borders" on page 54.)

Creating three-dimensional boxes (page 14)

If you own Adobe Dimensions, you can create a three-dimensional box by importing artwork from Adobe Illustrator and mapping it onto a box using the Artwork Mapping feature in Adobe Dimensions. When creating the artwork for the box, be sure to make guides for the outer edges of the box to help you align the graphics in Dimensions.

To create a true isometric view, first switch to Front view with a perspective of None. Then use the Rotate dialog box for the following two operations:

1. Click the Local button. Rotate the *y* axis 45°.
Click Apply.

2. Click the Global button. Rotate the *x* axis 35.3°.
Click Apply.

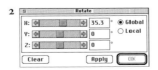

Creating a three-dimensional pie chart (page 16)

If you own Adobe Dimensions, you can make the pie chart three-dimensional. Create the pie chart in Adobe Illustrator, and paint each pie piece a different color. Import just the pie into Adobe Dimensions, choose an Off-Axis Top view angle, and extrude the pie. If you want to stagger the pie pieces, ungroup the pie after you import it. Select each pie piece and extrude it a different amount. You may need to choose a different view or revolve the graphic to view the staggered pieces. Adjust the lighting and surface properties, make sure that you've entered enough blend steps to avoid banding, and choose Shaded Render. Export the pie to an Illustrator file; then add type to complete the chart.

Unstaggered pieces

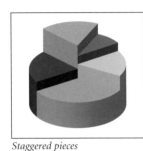
Staggered pieces

Creating a three-dimensional bar chart (page 18)

If you own Adobe Dimensions, you can create a three-dimensional graph design. Create the artwork in Adobe Illustrator; then import it into Dimensions and extrude it. Adjust the lighting and surface properties, and then export the artwork to an Illustrator file. Eliminate any surfaces that are completely hidden to keep the file size at a minimum and decrease the printing time. Then continue with step 10.

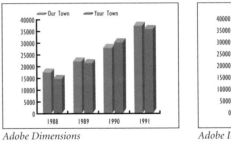
Adobe Dimensions   *Adobe Illustrator*

Shaded spherical objects (page 20)

If you own Adobe Dimensions, you can easily create spheres. However, because Adobe Dimensions adds black when it shades objects, you will not get precisely the same results as you will using the Photoshop technique. To create a multi-colored shadow on a sphere or to add texture as shown in the sample art of the eggs on page 20, use the technique as described in *Design Essentials.*

Adobe Dimensions

Adobe Photoshop

Drop shadows for objects (page 30)

If you are using Adobe Photoshop 2.5, you may be able to create the shadow or object shape more accurately using Quick Mask mode. If the object is difficult to select or has an intricate outline, switch to Quick Mask mode and use different brushes to touch up the selection edges. Then return to your artwork.

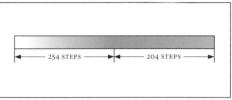

Linear spectrums (page 34)

If you're using Adobe Illustrator 5.0, you can easily create linear spectrums using the gradient fill tool. To create a rainbow arc like the one shown in the variation on page 35, however, use the blend tool as described in *Design Essentials*.

Full-color spectrums (page 36)

If you're using Adobe Photoshop 2.5, select the Clockwise Spectrum option in the Gradient Tool Options dialog box instead of selecting the HSB-CW color space in step 3. In the third step of the Enhancement, select the Normal option instead of the RGB/CMYK Color Space option.

Generating smooth blends (page 38)

While the new gradient fill tool in Adobe Illustrator 5.0 simplifies the creation of color blends and produces more reliable results, the general principles in this section still apply. You will still get banding if you use the wrong resolution/line screen combination, if the percent change from the beginning to the end of the blend is too small, if your gradient fill is too long, or if the blend is too dark relative to its length. Adobe Illustrator 5.0 does not display a recommended number of steps with the gradient fill tool. Therefore, to use the chart on page 39 of *Design Essentials*, you must calculate the recommended number of steps using the formula on page 40:

Number of steps = Number of grays × Percent change in color

See "Using Formulas for Special Cases" on page 40 of *Design Essentials* for complete information on how to calculate these variables. In addition, if you want to use the procedure described on page 41 and your gradient fill has been created in Adobe Illustrator 5.0, you must first save the file in Adobe Illustrator 3.0 format. Adobe Illustrator then converts the gradient fill to a shape blend that can be read by Adobe Photoshop, and calculates the number of steps necessary for each starting and ending color in the gradient fill. This means that if your gradient fill contains more than two colors, you could end up with more than 256 steps in the blend, which would result in a very large file size. For example, if your original gradient fill consists of a blend from white to green and then to aqua, Adobe Illustrator calculates the number of steps needed between white and green and then adds that to the number of steps needed between green and aqua.

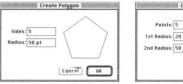

Adobe Illustrator 5.0 gradient fill

Same gradient fill opened in Adobe Illustrator 3.0

Constructing polygons for patterns (page 46)

If you are using Adobe Illustrator 5.0, you can create polygons automatically using the Create Polygon filter. You can also create stars automatically using the Create Star filter.

Gradations in type (page 62)

If you are using Adobe Illustrator 5.0, you can simply fill the type with any gradient fill using the Paint Style palette. You can then use the gradient fill tool to change the direction of the gradient fill or to create a single, continuous blend across all selected letters.

Default gradient fill direction　　*Direction changed using gradient fill tool*

Building a color palette for color posterization (tip on page 73)

If you are using Adobe Photoshop 2.5, you can save and load color palettes using the commands in the Colors palette menu. The Save Colors command saves the current palette in a file; the Load Colors command replaces the contents of the Colors palette with a stored palette.

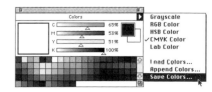

Additional Adobe Illustrator and Adobe Photoshop tips

Software needed: Adobe Illustrator 5.0; Adobe Photoshop 2.5

Quick grids in Adobe Illustrator

1. This procedure works with Adobe Illustrator 3.0 or higher. You can create grids very quickly if you know the number of grid boxes you want vertically and horizontally. Use the rectangle tool to create a rectangle. Don't worry about making it the right size or proportion for the page. You will adjust the size in step 8.

2. With the selection tool, begin dragging the rectangle to the right; then hold down the Shift and Option keys to constrain the movement and create a copy. When the rectangle is positioned as you want it, release the mouse button and then the Shift and Option keys.

3. Choose Repeat Transform from the Arrange menu (⌘D) as many times as necessary to create the number of boxes you want horizontally in your grid.

4. Select the entire row of rectangles.

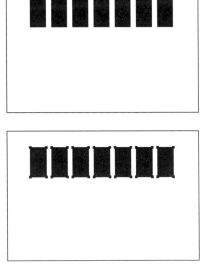

5. With the selection tool, begin dragging the rectangles downward; then hold down the Shift and Option keys. When the second row of rectangles is positioned as you want it, release the mouse button and then the Shift and Option keys.

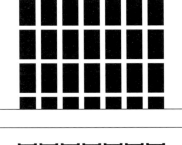

6. Choose Repeat Transform from the Arrange menu (⌘D) as many times as necessary to create the number of boxes you want vertically in your grid.

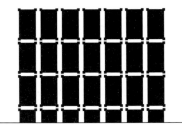

7. Select all of the boxes.

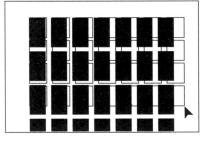

8. Select the scale tool, and click the upper left corner point of the grid to set the point of origin for the scale operation. Then drag from the upper left corner point to where you want the lower right corner of the grid.

9. With all boxes selected, choose Guides/Make from the Object menu (⌘5) to define the boxes as guides. (With Adobe Illustrator 3.0 or 4.0, choose Make Guide from the Arrange menu.)

❧ Creating fading lines in Adobe Illustrator

You can make a line or set of lines appear to fade using a filter and the gradient fill tool in Adobe Illustrator 5.0.

1. Create the lines that you want to appear to fade.

2. Select the lines, and choose Objects/Outline Stroked Path from the Filter menu.

3. In the Paint Style palette, select a gradient fill and fill the lines.

4. Use the gradient fill tool to adjust the angle of the fill to create the desired effect.

❧ Making tints of process color mixes in Adobe Illustrator

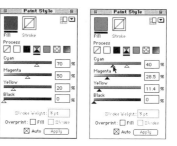

Often when you use a process color mix in your artwork, you also want to use a tint, or percentage, of the color. To create a tint in earlier versions of Illustrator, it was necessary to first convert the mix to a custom color. To create a tint of a process color mix in Adobe Illustrator 5.0, simply hold down the Shift key and drag any one of the Cyan, Magenta, Yellow, and Black slider triangles in the Paint Style palette. Dragging the sliders to the left produces a tint of the color. Dragging the sliders to the right produces a darker version of the color, up to 100% opacity of C, M, Y, or K.

❧ Using colors from your artwork to create gradient fills in Adobe Illustrator

You can copy colors directly from Adobe Illustrator artwork into your gradient fills. Open the file containing the colors you want in your gradient fill. In the Gradient dialog box, select the leftmost triangle beneath the gradient fill bar. Then select the eyedropper tool, hold down the Control key, and click any color in the artwork to copy the color into the gradient fill. You can use this proceure to add any number of colors to your gradient fill.

❧ Reverting selections in Adobe Photoshop

A useful feature in Adobe Photoshop 2.5.1 or higher lets you restore individual selections to the version last saved with the image. To use this feature, first make sure that your selection is active. Then choose Fill from the Edit menu, and choose Saved from the Use menu in the Fill dialog box. You can also adjust the opacity of the restored selection to create a double-exposure effect.

∾ Adjusting floating selections in Adobe Photoshop

Using painting and pasting modes. You can use the Brushes palette to experiment with and quickly preview the effects of the same painting modes and opacity levels available in the Fill and Composite Controls dialog boxes. To be affected by the Brushes palette controls, the selection must be floating. Make a selection, and choose Float from the Select menu (⌘J). Fill the selection or add a special effect such as a blend or a filter. Choose any of selection tools, and open the Brushes palette. Using the Mode menu in the Brushes palette, change the mode from Normal to Multiply, or choose Dissolve and adjust the opacity. This technique provides a quick way to use the painting and pasting modes any time the Brushes palette is open. Remember not to deselect the floating selection until the effect is as you want it.

Dodge and burn effects. You can use the same technique with the dodge and burn tools to modify the dodging or burning effect. Create a floating selection and apply the dodge or burn tool. Then choose any selection tool and change the Mode or opacity in the Brushes palette for different effects.

Dissolving type. To create the effect of dissolving type, create the type in Adobe Photoshop. Because type in Photoshop is created as a floating selection, you can use the Brushes palette options to modify the type until the type is deselected. Choose Dissolve from the Mode menu in the Brushes palette. To create the effect of dissolving edges only, keep the opacity at 100%. To create the effect of dissolving edges and a semitransparent, textured letterform, choose a lower opacity.

∾ Working on other projects during filter operations

When applying a complex filter to an image, it's not necessary to wait for the watch icon or progress bar to disappear before continuing with other work. Simply select the Finder under the Adobe Photoshop icon in the upper right of your menu bar. You can then open any other program and work while the filter is being applied in the background.

∾ Using monotones in color files in Adobe Photoshop

You can add a monotone to a color file to create a colorized effect in a composite image or collage. First convert the image that you want to be a monotone to Duotone mode (the image must first be in Grayscale mode). In the Duotone Options dialog box, choose Monotone from the Type menu, and assign a process or a custom color to the entire image. Select the entire image, and paste it into the color image you want to print. If you have chosen a custom color for the monotone, the color is converted to its CMYK equivalents. The pasted image will retain the look of a monotone even though it is printed with more than one color.

Using the Adobe Photoshop Colors palette

Color photographs as palettes. To load colors from a Photoshop file into the Colors palette, first convert a photograph to Indexed Color mode, and choose Color Table from the Mode menu. Click the Save button to save the colors; then choose Load Colors from the Colors palette menu, and select the color table you just saved. The Colors palette displays all colors from the photograph in the palette swatches.

 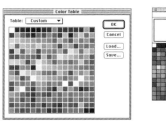 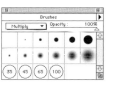

Color spectrums as palettes. You can easily create a full-color spectrum in the scratch pad using the gradient fill tool. Select the gradient fill tool, and choose Multiply from the Mode menu in the Brushes palette. Then apply the following gradients to the scratch pad:

1. Select 100% magenta, and drag from the upper left corner to the bottom right corner of the scratch pad.
2. Select 100% yellow, and drag from the lower left corner to the upper right corner of the pad.
3. Select 100% cyan, and drag from the upper right corner to the lower left of the pad.

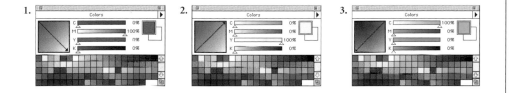

Custom patterns and brushes. To quickly create a pattern or brush without opening new file, draw or paint the pattern or brush shape on the scratch pad, and then use the rectangular marquee tool to select what you have drawn. Choose Define Pattern from the Edit menu to define the selection as a pattern; choose Define Brush from the Brushes palette menu to define the selection as a brush. Remember that you can define patterns as brushes and vice versa.

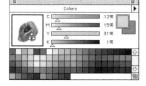

You can use any painting or selection tool in the Colors palette scratch pad. For example, you can copy part of an image directly into the palette using the Clone option of the rubber stamp tool. You can then use this cloned image as a color palette for a different image or to create a custom pattern or brush .

Modifying the palette swatches. Use these shortcuts to add colors to or subtract colors from the Colors palette:
- Hold down the Command key, and click to cut a color. (The scissors icon appears.)
- Hold down the Option key, and click to replace an existing color. (The paint bucket icon appears.)
- Hold down the Shift and Option keys, and click to insert a color and shift all existing colors one swatch to the right. (The paint bucket icon appears.)

Transparent type selections

Type created in Adobe Photoshop is always generated with the current foreground color inside the floating selection. In some situations, you may want to apply a filter to or otherwise modify the image beneath the selection. To remove the opaque foreground color, choose a selection tool while the type is still selected. Then set the opacity to 0% in the Brushes palette. The type bcomes a transparent selection. As long as it remains selected, you can move the type selection around without altering the pixels within it. To save the selection for later use, choose Save Selection from the Select menu.

Bibliography

ADOBE SYSTEMS INC. *Classroom in a Book: Adobe Illustrator.*
Mountain View, CA: Adobe Press/Hayden Books, 1993.

ADOBE SYSTEMS INC. *Classroom in a Book: Adobe Photoshop.*
Mountain View, CA: Adobe Press/Hayden Books, 1993.

ADOBE SYSTEMS INC. *Classroom in a Book: Adobe Premiere.*
Mountain View, CA: Adobe Press/Hayden Books, 1993.

ANDRES, CLAY. *Illustrator Illuminated.*
Berkeley, CA: Peachpit Press Inc., 1992.

BIEDNY, DAVID, AND BERT MONROY. *The Official Photoshop Handbook.*
New York: Bantam Books, 1991.

BRINGHURST, ROBERT. *The Elements of Typographic Style.*
Point Roberts, WA: Hartley and Marks, 1992.

BRUNO, MICHAEL. *Pocket Pal.*
15th ed. New York: International Paper Company, 1992.

COHEN, BROWN, JEANS, AND WENDLING. *Design Essentials.*
Mountain View, CA: Adobe Press/Hayden Books, 1992.

DAY, ROB. *Designer Photoshop.*
New York: Random House, 1993.

ENDO, ETSURO. *Adobe Photoshop A to Z.*
Tokyo: Bug News Network, 1993.

FIELD, GARY G. *Color and Its Reproduction.*
Pittsburgh, PA: Graphic Arts Technical Foundation, 1988.

IGARASHI, TAKENOBU, AND DIANE BURNS. *Designers on Mac.*
Tokyo: Graphic-sha Publishing Company, 1992.

LAWLER, BRIAN. *The Color Resource Complete Guide to Trapping.*
San Francisco: The Color Resource, 1993.

MCCLELLAND, DEKE. *Mastering Adobe Illustrator.*
Homewood, IL: Business One Irwin, 1991.

MILLER, MARC D. AND RANDY ZAUCHA. *The Color Mac.*
Carmel, IN: Hayden Books, 1992.

RICH, JIM, AND SANDY BOZEK. *Adobe Photoshop 2.5 in Black and White.*
Annapolis, MD: Bozek Desktop Inc., 1993.

SOUTHWORTH, MILES, THAD MCILROY, AND DONNA SOUTHWORTH.
The Color Resource Complete Color Glossary.
San Francisco: The Color Resource, 1992.

SPIEKERMANN, ERIK, AND E. M. GINGER. *Stop Stealing Sheep & Find Out How Type Works.*
Mountain View, CA: Adobe Press/Hayden Books, 1993.

Index

Colophon

This book was designed and produced using Adobe Illustrator, Adobe Photoshop, Adobe Dimensions, Adobe Premiere, Adobe Type Manager™, and QuarkXPress® on a Macintosh IIfx. The Adobe Original typefaces Minion™ and Minion Expert, designed by Robert Slimbach, are used throughout the book.

Final film was printed at 175 lines per inch on a Adobe/Scitex® RIP and Scitex Dolev™ Imagesetter by Metagraphics, Palo Alto, California.

The book was printed by Shepard Poorman, Indianapolis, Indiana.

Other Titles From Adobe Press

Adobe Press publishes several other books that will augment your understanding of Adobe's powerful software applications and advanced technologies. Written and developed by Adobe Systems and published by Hayden Books of Prentice Hall Computer Publishing, these books are available at your local computer book bookseller, or you may order direct from Prentice Hall by calling 1-800-428-5331.

The best-selling **Design Essentials**, by Luanne Cohen, Russell Brown, Lisa Jeans, and Tanya Wendling, is the perfect companion to *Imaging Essentials*. **Design Essentials** provides illustrated, step-by-step procedures for creating graphic and photographic effects using Adobe Illustrator and Adobe Photoshop. "The insider's guide to all the tricks of Adobe. This book never leaves my desk. A must-have for all designers!" Mary K. Baumann, Hopkins/Baumann
ISBN: 0-672-48538-9 112 pages,
$39.95 U.S.A., $49.95 Canada

PostScript Screening: Adobe Accurate Screens, by Peter Fink, is the first and only book that explains the screening technology that is a standard part of the PostScript language in a graphic arts prepress and print production context. "*PostScript Screening* is the best introduction to the whole subject of visual screening, halftones, and so forth, that I have yet seen."
Jerry Pournelle, *BYTE Magazine*
ISBN: 0-672-48544-3 176 pages,
$24.95 U.S.A., $31.95 Canada

Stop Stealing Sheep & find out how type works, by Erik Spiekermann and E. M. Ginger, is the most lively and accessible book on type available. This colorful and unique guidebook provides a common-sense explanation of what type is and how to use it effectively as a powerful communications tool. A book for all levels of computer users. "The most intellectually stimulating book on type recently, *Stop Stealing Sheep* weds graphic excitement with literary accomplishment." AIGA
ISBN: 0-672-48543-5 176 pages,
$19.95 U.S.A., $24.95 Canada

Beyond Paper: Adobe Acrobat, by Patrick Ames, paints a colorful overview of the features of Adobe Acrobat™ software by comparing how you work today with how you might work tomorrow. Written for computer users of all levels. **Beyond Paper** will help you understand this newest technology that will change the face of publishing, if you use a computer to create documents that other people read or view.
ISBN: 1-56830-050-6 128 pages,
$16.95 U.S.A., $21.95 Canada

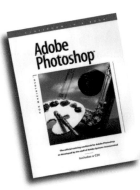

The newest series from Adobe Press is the **Classroom in a Book** series, which covers Adobe Illustrator, Adobe Photoshop, and Adobe Premiere for both the Macintosh and Windows platforms. These unique and hands-on workbooks guide the reader through self-paced training lessons and tutorials in a way no other book or training class could, because all of the lesson files are included on a CD-ROM disc included with the book. Designed and tested in Adobe's classrooms, even the most accomplished power user will benefit in just a few hours. Each **Classroom in a Book** retails for $44.95. U.S.A., $56.95 Canada, is 256 pages long, and includes a CD/ROM disc.
Adobe Photoshop, Macintosh: ISBN: 1-56830-055-7
Adobe Photoshop, Windows: ISBN: 1-56830-054-9
Adobe Premiere, Macintosh: ISBN: 1-56830-052-2
Adobe Illustrator, Macintosh: ISBN: 1-56830-056-5
Adobe Illustrator, Windows: ISBN: 1-56830-053-0